TOM SWIFT
AND THE
ELECTRONIC
HYDROLUNG

VICTOR APPLETON

1st WORLD
LIBRARY
Literary Society

Tom Swift and the Electronic Hydrolung

Victor Appleton

© 1st World Library, 2006
PO Box 2211
Fairfield, IA 52556
www.1stworldlibrary.com
First Edition

LCCN: 2006935360

Softcover ISBN: 1-4218-2505-8
Hardcover ISBN: 1-4218-2405-1
eBook ISBN: 1-4218-2605-4

Purchase *"Tom Swift and the Electronic Hydrolung"*
as a traditional bound book at:
www.1stWorldLibrary.com/purchase.asp?ISBN=1-4218-2505-8

1st World Library is a literary, educational organization
dedicated to:

- Creating a free internet library of downloadable ebooks

- Hosting writing competitions and offering book
publishing scholarships.

Interested in more 1st World Library books?
contact: literacy@1stworldlibrary.com
Check us out at: www.1stworldlibrary.com

1ˢᵗ World Library Literary Society

Giving Back to the World

"If you want to work on the core problem, it's early school literacy."

- James Barksdale, former CEO of Netscape

"No skill is more crucial to the future of a child, or to a democratic and prosperous society, than literacy."

- Los Angeles Times

Literacy... means far more than learning how to read and write... The aim is to transmit... knowledge and promote social participation."

- UNESCO

"Literacy is not a luxury, it is a right and a responsibility. If our world is to meet the challenges of the twenty-first century we must harness the energy and creativity of all our citizens."

- President Bill Clinton

"Parents should be encouraged to read to their children, and teachers should be equipped with all available techniques for teaching literacy, so the varying needs and capacities of individual kids can be taken into account."

- Hugh Mackay

CONTENTS

CHAPTER I

PIRATE MISSILE

Tense, excited men gazed spaceward from the ships and planes of the South Atlantic task force. Other watchers waited breathlessly in the control room of the ship *Recoverer*. Among these was Tom Swift Jr.

"How close to earth is our Jupiter probe missile?" Bud Barclay asked Tom excitedly.

The lanky blond youth beside him, in T shirt and slacks, shot a glance at the dials of the tracking equipment. "Eight thousand miles from this spot, Bud. It should land here in fifteen minutes!"

Tom Jr., his father, Bud, and a host of scientists, Navy officers, and newsmen were crowded aboard a U.S. Navy missile launching ship.

"Just think!" Bud exulted. "You'll have data from the planet Jupiter that no one on earth has yet been able to get!"

"*If* we recover the missile safely," Mr. Swift spoke up hopefully. The elder scientist's voice was quiet but taut with the strain of waiting. The two Swifts resembled each other closely - each had deep-set blue eyes and clean-cut features - although Tom was somewhat taller and rangier.

"You're right, Dad," Tom agreed. "If we don't snare the missile, our whole project will be a total loss to America's space program!"

At Tom's words, the watchers and crewmen who were crowded into the *Recoverer*'s control room stirred restlessly. Its bulkheads were banked with radar and telemetering devices. Tension had been mounting throughout the morning aboard the ships and observation planes of the ask force as everyone awaited the return of the planet-circling missile - scientists' deepest penetration into space so far.

"What do you mean, a total loss?" Bud argued. "Even if the recovery operation's a flop, the shot will still pay off in valuable information, won't it?"

Tom shook his head grimly. "The purpose of this unmanned, exploratory flight around Jupiter was to take and record all kinds of data. But none of the info is being radioed back to us."

"How come?"

"If we had put in radio gear strong enough to relay signals back, it would have cut down the amount of information-gathering equipment aboard," Tom explained. "We had to make every ounce count."

Outwardly calm, Tom was seething with inner excitement. Although only eighteen - the same age as his husky, dark-haired pal and copilot, Bud Barclay - Tom had been given the job of directing the recovery phase of the United States government's Project Jupiter survey. The Swifts and their rocket research staff had built the missile and engineered the space probe for the government.

"Whew!" Bud gave a nervous whistle. "I see what you mean, pal. With all our eggs in one basket, we sure can't afford to get butter-fingered with the Jupiter prober."

Victor Appleton

Admiral Walter, a tall, distinguished man, graying at the temples, smiled. "It's what we call in warfare a calculated risk, Bud," he said. "But with Tom in charge, I believe we have nothing to worry about."

Mr. Swift's eyes shone with fatherly pride at the admiral's remark. Tom Jr.'s pioneering rocket flights and inventions had won the youth a top rank in American space research.

"Guess you're right, sir," Bud agreed. "I'll back genius boy here any day!"

Tom winced as Bud whacked him heartily on the shoulder. "Better save your orchids and keep your fingers crossed, fly boy," the young inventor advised. "That rocket's not home yet."

Radio telescopes, both on land and aboard the ships of the task force, were following the missile's progress as it drew closer to earth. All were feeding a steady stream of information to the ships' computers.

"How soon will you fire the retro-rockets, Tom?" Admiral Walter inquired presently.

"In about ten seconds, sir," Tom replied, eying the sweep second hand of the clock.

Moments later, a red light flashed on the master control panel. Tom's finger stabbed a button. Far out in space, the retarding rockets in the missile's nose were triggered for a brief burst, slowing its high speed. Without this, the missile would hurtle to flaming destruction in the atmosphere.

"We've picked it up!" shouted a radarman.

Bud gave a whoop of excitement and everyone crowded around the radarscope. Tom's steel-blue eyes checked the blip. Then he threw a switch which started an automatic plotting machine that had been prepared with the landing plan, and noted that the missile was slightly off the correct path. A new flow of information now began pulsing in as other ships' tracking radars recorded its course. The data was being fed automatically to the "capture" computer. This would analyze the correct flight path for the recovery missile, which would magnetically seize the returning traveler from Jupiter and bring it safely home.

Tom quickly read off the results from the computer's dials, then busied himself again with the retarding-rocket controls.

"Everything going okay, skipper?" Bud asked.

Tom nodded. "I've readjusted the retarding rockets. They'll fire at the proper intervals to slow down the missile still further and bring it back on beam."

The excited buzz of voices in the compartment gradually quieted as the clock ticked steadily toward the next step in the recovery operation.

"Stand by for missile firing!" Tom snapped.

A seaman relayed the order over the ship's intercom. Tense silence fell as Tom's eyes followed the sweep of the second hand.

"All clear for blast-off!" came the talker's report.

Tom pressed the firing button. A split second later the listeners' eardrums throbbed to a muffled roar from topside as the slender recovery missile shot skyward. The ship rocked convulsively from the shock of blast-off. Then it steadied again as the gyros damped out the vibrations.

"Wow!" Bud heaved a sigh of relieved tension. Then he dashed from the compartment and up the nearest ladder for a quick look at the rocket as it disappeared into the blue.

Tom watched the recovery missile intently on the radarscope.

"Nice going, son," said Mr. Swift quietly.

In response to his father's reassuring grip on his arm, Tom flashed him a hasty smile. For the first time, the young inventor realized he was beaded with perspiration and that his pulse was hammering.

"It's a case of wait and hope," Tom murmured.

On every ship and plane in the task force, eyes were glued to the radar screens. Two small blips were visible - one the Jupiter probe missile, the other the recovery missile - moving on courses that would soon intersect.

Just as Bud returned to the compartment, several of the watchers gave startled gasps.

"Another blip - coming in from nine o'clock!" Admiral Walter exclaimed. "What's that?"

Tom stared at the new blip. It was moving steadily toward the meeting point of the first two missiles!

"It's a thief missile!" Tom cried out. "Some enemy's trying to steal our probe data!"

"Good night!" Bud gulped. "Who'd dare try that?"

"I don't know," Tom muttered tensely. "But if those three missiles meet, our whole project will be wrecked!"

"Better tape all readings!" Mr. Swift advised.

"Right, Dad!"

Admiral Walter had paled slightly under his deep tan. In stunned silence, the Navy officers and scientists watched as

Tom's lean hands manipulated two controls.

"What are those for?" Bud asked.

"One's to speed up our recovery missile," Tom explained. "Looks like a slim hope, though, from the way that third blip is homing on target. This other control has just caused every instrument on this ship, and all the others in the task force, to make permanent records on magnetic tape of all their readings.

"If a collision occurs and the probe missile falls into the sea," Tom went on, "there's only one hope of recovery - to plot the exact geographical position and then get to the spot before the enemy does!"

"Roger!" Bud agreed.

It was obvious that Tom's fears about the missiles colliding were well founded. The mystery blip had veered as the recovery missile speeded up. Within seconds, the three blips met on the screen and fused into a single spot of light.

"The probe missile's no longer responding to control!" one of the telemetering scientists called out.

Admiral Walter, grim-faced, flashed a questioning look at Tom. "Then recovery has failed?"

"I'm afraid so, sir."

The fused blip was still visible on screen as the radar dishes tracked it, moving in a way that indicated a steep downward plunge.

For a moment Tom felt numb with despair. But he set his jaw firmly and turned to the admiral.

"Sir, I'd like helicopters readied for take-off immediately," Tom said. "As soon as the tracking instruments lose contact,

Victor Appleton

have the recording tapes picked up from every ship in the task force and brought here to the *Recoverer*."

Admiral Walter nodded tersely. "Very well. Then what?"

"I'll get to work right now," Tom replied, "and lay out a computer program to process the readings."

The data - consisting of millions of information "bits" from the shipboard instrument tapes - would be fed to an electronic brain. The brain would then calculate the probable location in latitude and longitude of the sunken missile.

As the admiral snapped out orders, Tom exchanged a brief worried glance with his father. Each was pondering the same thought.

Could Tom find the lost Jupiter probe missile? Or would their enemy locate it first?

CHAPTER II

UNDERSEA SURVEY

With an effort, Tom forced all thoughts of failure out of his mind and concentrated on the job at hand. In an hour he had the computer program blocked out.

Mr. Swift and several of the other scientists checked his work. Each nodded approval. By this time, the fused blip had long since disappeared from the radarscopes, indicating that the Jupiter probe missile - or what was left of it - had plunged to the ocean bottom.

"What's your next move, Tom?" Admiral Walter asked.

"No point in wasting time waiting for the computer results," Tom decided. "Suppose Bud and I fly back to Swift Enterprises and organize a search party."

"Good idea." As Admiral Walter extended a hand, his weather-beaten face softened. "And don't feel downhearted, son. You rate a Navy 'E' for the way you handled this operation. It would have succeeded if it hadn't been for that confounded enemy missile!"

"Thank you, sir." Tom managed a grateful grin, in spite of his discouragement.

Minutes later, the two boys embarked in a motor launch that

Victor Appleton

took them to an aircraft carrier standing by in the vicinity. From the flattop they took off in a Navy jet for Shopton.

Meanwhile, Mr. Swift remained aboard the *Recoverer* to supervise the data processing. Tom, looking back from the soaring jet, could see one of the helicopters on its way to the missile ship to deliver the first batch of tapes.

It was late afternoon when the Navy jet touched down on the Enterprises airfield. The Swifts' sprawling experimental station was a walled, four-mile-square enclosure with landing strips, work-shops, and laboratories, near the town of Shopton. Here Tom Jr. and his father developed their amazing inventions.

Tom and Bud hopped into a jeep at the hangar and sped to the Administration Building, where Tom shared a double office with his father. Bud sank down into one of the deep-cushioned leather chairs, while Tom adjusted the Venetian blinds to let in the afternoon sunshine.

The spacious office was furnished with twin modern desks, conference table, and drawing boards which swung out from wall slots at the press of a button. At one end of the room were the video screen and control board of the Swifts' private TV network. Here and there stood scale models of their inventions, a huge relief globe of the earth, and a replica of the planet Mars.

"What are your plans for our search expedition, skipper?" Bud asked.

Tom ran his fingers through his crew cut. "Let's see. We'd better take the *Sky Queen*, I think, and also -"

Tom broke off as the desk intercom buzzed. Miss Trent, the Swifts' secretary, was on the wire.

"Your father's calling over the radio, Tom."

"Swell!" Tom flicked a switch to cut in the signal of his private telephone. "Hi, Dad! We just got back. Any news?"

"Yes, son. We have the computer results," Mr. Swift replied. "Got a pencil handy?"

Tom copied down the latitude and longitude figures as his father dictated.

"According to the latest hydrographic maps, based on IGY findings," Mr. Swift went on, "this area is a high plateau of the Atlantic Ridge - it's near the St. Paul Rocks."

"What about the depth?"

"It averages between a hundred and three hundred feet," said the elder scientist.

Tom gave a whistle. "Lucky break, eh?"

"Maybe and maybe not," Mr. Swift said cautiously. "The bottom there is heavily silted."

"Oh - oh." Tom made a wry face. "In that case, we may have some digging to do."

"I'm afraid so. However, no use borrowing trouble." After a short discussion, the elder scientist added, "I'll probably fly home tomorrow, son. Give my love to Mother and Sandy."

"Right, Dad. So long!" Tom hung up and reported the news to Bud.

"What kind of underwater gear will we use?" Bud inquired.

"I'm not sure myself," Tom admitted. "Guess we'll have to take along a variety of equipment and play it by ear."

Before proceeding with his search plans, Tom phoned home to

inform his mother of his arrival. Mrs. Swift was sympathetic when she heard of the failure to recover the probe missile.

"I'm sure you'll locate it," she said encouragingly.

"Some of your cooking will sure help brighten the picture," Tom replied with a grin. As he put down the receiver a moment later, he told Bud, "You're having dinner with us tonight, pal. Fried chicken and biscuits."

Bud licked his lips. "Lead me to it!"

Chuckling, Tom began drawing up a list of supplies for the expedition. Bud helped with the details, after which Tom phoned the underground hangar and the Swifts' rocket base at Fearing Island to give the orders for the next day. Crewmen were also detailed for the trip.

It was six o'clock when the two boys finally piled into Tom's low-slung sports car and drove to the Swifts' big, pleasant house on the outskirts of Shopton. Sandra, Tom's blond, vivacious sister, greeted them at the door.

"About time!" she teased. "We were beginning to think you two had taken off somewhere."

"Think I'd leave town while you and that fried chicken are in Shopton?" Bud grinned.

"What a line!" Sandy's blue eyes twinkled. "I know it's the fried chicken you're really interested in."

"Where's the rest of that 'we' you were referring to?" Tom inquired.

"I'm sorry, Tom," Sandy said in a mournful voice. "Phyl couldn't make it."

As Tom's face fell, she burst out giggling and a second later

Phyllis Newton emerged from the kitchen. Brown-eyed, with long dark hair, Phyl was the daughter of Tom Sr.'s old comrade-in-arms and lifelong chum "Uncle Ned" Newton. Like Sandy, she was seventeen.

"You didn't think I'd miss this rare evening, did you, Tom?" she said, laughing. "After all, it isn't often we see you two."

Sandy and Phyl liked to needle the boys about their infrequent dates, due to Tom's and Bud's busy schedules.

Mrs. Swift, slender and sweet-faced, gave Tom a hug and greeted Bud warmly. Over the delicious dinner, the conversation turned to the mysterious thief missile.

"Who on earth could have fired it?" Sandy asked.

Tom shrugged. "No telling - yet. There's more than one unfriendly country which would give a lot for the data picked up on our Jupiter shot."

"You aren't expecting more trouble, are you?" Phyl put in uneasily.

Tom passed the question off lightly in order not to alarm his mother and the two girls. But inwardly he was none too sure of what his survey expedition might encounter in trying to locate the lost probe missile.

Ever since his first adventure in his Flying Lab, the youthful inventor had been involved in many daring exploits and thrilling situations. Time and again, Tom had had to combat enemy spies and vicious plotters bent on stealing the Swifts' scientific secrets.

His research projects had taken him far into outer space and into the depths of the ocean. With his atomic earth blaster, Tom had probed under the earth's crust at the South Pole, and in other adventures he had faced danger in the jungles of

Africa, New Guinea, and Yucatan. His latest achievement, receiving the visitor from Planet X, had been to construct a robot body for this mysterious brain energy from another world. Now, Tom realized, he was on the brink of another adventure which might hold unexpected dangers.

Early the next morning the majestic *Sky Queen* was hoisted from its underground hangar berth and hauled by tractor to its special runway. This mammoth, atomic-powered airplane had been Tom's first major invention. A three-deck craft, it was equipped with complete laboratory facilities for research in any corner of the globe. Jet lifters in the belly of the fuselage enabled the craft to take off vertically and also to hover.

As Tom supervised the loading of the equipment, a foghorn voice boomed, "'Mornin', buckaroos!"

The chunky figure of Chow Winkler came into view. Formerly a chuck-wagon cook in Texas, Chow was now head chef on Tom's expeditions. As usual, a ten-gallon hat was perched on his balding head and he was stomping along in high-heeled boots.

"Wow! A shirt to end all shirts!" Tom chuckled.

"Real high style, eh?" Chow twirled about to display his latest Western creation. The shirt seemed to be made of silvery fishlike scales, which glistened like a rainbow.

"I figured as how this was just the thing fer an ocean jaunt," Chow added with a grin. "How soon do we take off, boss?"

"As soon as we get the rest of this gear stowed," Tom replied.

Twenty minutes later the *Sky Queen* soared toward the ocean. Soon they came in sight of Fearing Island rocket base, a few miles off the coast. Once a barren stretch of sand dunes and scrub-grass, the island was now the Swifts' top-secret rocket laboratory, guarded by drone planes and radar. It served as the supply base for Tom's space station and as the launching area for all space flights. Seacopters and jetmarines were also berthed here.

A radio call from Tom brought a sleek, strange-looking craft zooming up to join them.

It was the *Sea Hound*, latest and largest model of Tom's amazing diving seacopter. It had an enclosed central rotor, powered by atomic turbines, with reversible-pitch blades for air lift or undersea diving. Superheated steam jets provided forward propulsion in either element.

As the *Sea Hound* streaked alongside the Flying Lab, two figures in the seacopter's flight compartment waved to Tom and Bud. One was Hank Sterling, the blond, square-jawed chief pattern-making engineer of Enterprises. The other was husky Arv Hanson, a talented craftsman who transformed the blueprints of Tom's inventions into working models.

"All set," Hank radioed. "Lead the way."

"Roger!" Tom replied.

Flying at supersonic speed, they reached the area of the lost missile in the South Atlantic soon after lunch. Already on hand were ships of the Navy task force assigned by Admiral Walter to participate in the missile search. The *Sea Hound* settled down on the surface of the water, while the *Sky Queen* hovered at low altitude nearby.

Tom contacted the government craft and learned that as yet no sign of the lost Jupiter prober had been detected. Then he made ready to begin his own search.

"Let's try the Fat Man suits first," Tom told Bud. Turning to Slim Davis, a Swift test pilot who was in the crew, the young inventor added, "Take over, will you, Slim?"

"Righto." Slim eased into the pilot's seat.

"Got a job for me, skipper?" asked Doc Simpson, Swift Enterprises' young medic.

"Yes. Help the boys, if you like, rig the undersea elevator, and then assemble a tractorized air dome," Tom suggested.

"Will do," Doc promised.

A ladder was dropped. Tom and Bud excitedly descended to the *Sea Hound*. The search for the lost missile was about to begin!

Once the boys were aboard, the seacopter submerged and dived quickly to the ocean floor. Tom and Bud each climbed into a Fat Man suit and went out through the air lock. The suits, shaped like huge steel eggs with a quartz-glass view plate for the operator seated within, had mechanical arms and legs.

The boys waddled about, the built-in searchlights of their suits piercing the murky gloom. They saw nothing but the deep accumulation of silt on the ocean bottom, which made the going difficult.

"This is too slow," Tom called over his sonarphone. "Let's try the air dome."

The dome was a huge underwater bubble of air, created by a repelatron device which actually pushed the ocean water away. The air supply inside was kept pure by one of Tom's osmotic air conditioners which made use of the oxygen dissolved in the water.

The air bubble, however, even with its jet-propelled platform, also proved inadequate for the research job. Its caterpillar treads repeatedly bogged down in the silt.

"Maybe the seacopter itself is our best bet," Bud suggested.

"Worth a try," Tom urged.

But the *Sea Hound*, too, had a serious drawback. Even with its powerful search beam sweeping the ocean floor as it prowled along, the explorers found their vision too limited.

Finally Tom said, "Bud, we could skin-dive at this depth."

"Let's give it a whirl," Bud urged.

The seacopter surfaced again, while the boys donned flippers, masks, and air lungs. Then they dropped over the side and made their way slowly downward into the gray-green depths, accustoming themselves gradually to the increased pressure.

"A lot more freedom of action," Tom thought. "If only we didn't have to communicate by signals!"

There was a sudden *swoosh* somewhere on his right. A projectile, Tom realized! Turning, his eyes widened in horror as he saw an uprush of bubbles.

Bud's air tank had been hit!

CHAPTER III

INVISIBLE SUB

Without wasting a moment, Tom lunged through the water toward his stricken friend. Bud was floundering and thrashing about weakly. He seemed dazed by the sudden shock of his plight.

"Or maybe the impact of the projectile stunned him!" Tom surmised.

Bud began groping his way upward just as Tom came alongside of him. Tom grabbed him as best he could, hooking onto his belt. At the same time, the young inventor inhaled deeply, yanked out Bud's useless mouthpiece, and inserted his own in its place.

Bud's eyes glowed with gratitude.

"We'll have to get topside fast," Tom thought, "even though it means risking the bends."

He stroked upward and they shot toward the surface. Bud assisted to some extent, partly revived by the gulp of air.

As they rose, fathom by fathom, their progress seemed to grow maddeningly slower. Tom had to let air bubbles escape constantly from his mouth. As the pressure decreased, due to the lessening depth of the water, the air in his lungs expanded and he was forced to breathe out.

Tom noticed with dismay that Bud was not responding very well, his feeble strokes were jerky and uncoordinated. "Must've lost pressure too fast when his tank was hit," Tom realized.

The water was growing greener and brighter now as they neared the sunshine. The *Sea Hound*'s shadowy outline loomed just above. With a last desperate burst of strength, Tom lunged upward and they broke water.

"H-h-help!" Tom gasped.

There was no need for the cry. Hank and his crew, on the seacopter's forward deck, had already grasped the situation. Strong arms reached out and hauled the two boys aboard.

Both of them were shivering and writhing in pain, only half conscious.

"They have the bends!" Arv Hanson cried in alarm. "Signal the *Sky Queen* to drop a sling!"

The boys' masks were ripped off. Within moments, Bud had been tightly secured to the sling, which was reeled back up into the plane. Tom followed in a few minutes. Doc Simpson took charge of the patients immediately. After a quick examination, he had the boys placed in a small decompression chamber in the *Sky Queen*'s sick bay.

"How are they?" Hank asked anxiously as he peered through the window of the chamber. The medic had given Bud a sedative and he was already fast
asleep. Tom remained awake.

"Aside from the pain, not in too bad shape," Doc Simpson replied.

It turned out that Tom's case was not so serious, but Bud had

Victor Appleton

to stay in bed. With Tom, it was only a matter of decompression and he soon was up and about.

Chow, in a chef's cap, with an apron around his paunchy stomach, had come stomping in hastily from the galley. "Pore lil ole boys," he fussed. "Brand my snorkel, I never should've let you young'uns go pokin' around down below there without me around to keep an eye on things!"

Tom slapped the loyal old Texan on the back. "If you want a dive, come along."

"You're goin' back down?" Chow asked.

"In the seacopter," Tom replied. "To find out, if possible, who fired that projectile at us."

"Then count me in!" Chow declared, stripping off his apron. "I just hope I get my hands on them sneakin' polecats!"

Slim Davis would pilot the *Sky Queen* back to Shopton at once, because of Bud. Tom and Chow, meanwhile, would join Hank and his crew aboard the *Sea Hound*.

Ten minutes later the sleek seacopter, its searchlight off to avoid detection, was plummeting downward through water that changed before their eyes from greenish blue to a deep-gray gloom. Iridescent fish darted past the cabin window.

"Think the enemy sub was searching for our Jupiter prober?" Hank asked.

"It must have been," Tom reasoned.

Hank frowned. "Which means they must have figured out the missile's position as fast as our side did."

"And they'll play rough to stop us from finding it," Arv added forebodingly.

Within moments, the group clustered in the pilot's cabin felt a gentle bump as the *Sea Hound* settled on the submerged plateau. Tom relaxed at the controls but kept the rotors going so the craft would remain submerged. Meanwhile, the sonarman was probing the surrounding waters.

"Any pings?" Tom asked.

The man shook his head without taking his eyes from the sonarscope. "Nothing yet."

Hank Sterling donned a hydrophone headset and listened intently. The silence deepened in the *Sea Hound*'s cabin. Suddenly Hank stiffened and the sonarman cried out:

"A blip, skipper! At two o'clock!"

It was moving rapidly on the scope - something streaking toward their starboard beam!

"Good night! It's another missile!" Tom gasped.

He darted back to the controls and gunned the reverse jets just in time! The missile flashed across their bow.

"Great bellowin' longhorns!" Chow gasped weakly. His leathery face had gone pale under its tan. "The yellow-livered drygulchers!"

"I don't get it," Arv Hanson spoke up. "If they're in firing range, we should have detected them, shouldn't we?"

Tom nodded grimly. "Whoever our enemies are, they must have perfected a way to make themselves invisible to underwater detection.

"*And we'll have to do the same!*" he vowed inwardly. Aloud, Tom said, "I hate to run from those sneaks, but if we stick around, we'll be asking for trouble."

Victor Appleton

Slowing the rotors to permit the craft to rise, Tom guided the *Sea Hound* back to the surface. Then he reversed blade pitch for air flight and gunned the atomic turbines. The seacopter rose steeply above the billowing South Atlantic.

Tom radioed a terse report of their experience to the task-force commander and in turn was told that none of the naval craft had either sighted or picked up any sign of a strange sub.

As they streaked homeward, Chow was still fuming. "Why don't we post a dummy sub there to scare off the varmints?"

"I'll pass the idea along to the Navy," Tom said with a grin.

Night had fallen when the searchers arrived back at Fearing Island. Tom cleared with the tower and landed, then went by jeep to base headquarters. He called Enterprises and learned that Bud's condition was improved, and that Mr. Swift had returned that afternoon. He spoke to him about the mystery sub.

"This is bad news indeed, son," Mr. Swift said, after hearing how the attacker had defied detection. "You'd better inform Admiral Walter. He had to fly back to Washington."

"I'll call him right away," Tom promised.

The admiral was equally disturbed when Tom succeeded in reaching him. "We must find that missile as soon as possible - at any cost," he said. "Tom, you Swifts have had considerable experience in undersea dredging. Could you send a team of engineers to assist us in the work?"

"Yes, sir," the young inventor replied. "I'll assign men to the job first thing tomorrow."

After hanging up, Tom hopped back to the mainland with Chow in a Pigeon Special. This sleek little commercial plane was manufactured by the Swift Construction Company in charge of Ned Newton.

Early the next morning Tom and his father drove to Enterprises, and the young inventor plunged into the job of organizing an engineering crew for the missile hunt. Art Wiltessa, a crack underwater specialist as well as engineer, was placed in charge.

By noon the group had taken off for the South Atlantic in a Swift cargo jet. A small portable model of Tom's atomic earth blaster was included in their equipment. A jetmarine and a diving seacopter were also dispatched from Fearing to assist in the operations.

"It's apt to be a long-drawn-out job - and dangerous," commented Mr. Swift as he lunched with Tom in their office.

"Yes. Digging in that silt could be almost as bad as working in quicksand."

Mr. Swift's deep-set blue eyes took on a thoughtful gleam. "Speaking of silt, son, I've found the ideal spot for my secret deep-sea farm."

"You mean for growing those plants you use in making Tomasite?" Tom asked.

The elder scientist nodded. Tomasite, a revolutionary plastic which Mr. Swift had developed, possessed amazing insulating properties against both heat and radiation. One of its secret ingredients came from certain plants found only in Far Eastern waters. Mr. Swift hoped to transplant them locally.

"The site is near Fearing Island - about fifty feet in depth," he added.

"You may have a tough time finding gardeners, Dad," Tom pointed out. "Men can't work that far down for very long at one time."

Victor Appleton

"It'll be a problem," Mr. Swift conceded. He finished his coffee, then looked up with a twinkle in his eyes. "How about figuring out a solution for me, Tom?"

"A new kind of air lung?" Tom was intrigued!

CHAPTER IV

AERIAL ATTACK

"Yes, son," Mr. Swift went on. "What's needed is a new type of breathing device - one that will eliminate bulky air tanks and permit a skin diver to stay down for long periods."

"Quite an order, Dad."

Grabbing a pencil, the young inventor began sketching. In both his Fat Man suits and his osmotic air conditioner, Tom had already perfected ways of drawing oxygen from sea water.

"But a small gadget for skin divers," he said, "will take a fantastic job of electronic miniaturization." After a pause he added, "It could really speed up recovery of the Jupiter prober, though."

Lunch over, Tom hopped a jet scooter and sped off to his private laboratory. The modernistic glass-walled structure - designed by Tom himself - had every tool of modern scientific research, from electronic microscope to helium cryostat.

As always, whenever he was absorbed in a new idea, Tom was eager to get to work. "Let's see what I'm shooting for. A small container, slung around the diver's neck?... No, too dangerous. Better hook it to his weight belt, with a tube to his face mask."

Using a plastic foam "breadboard," Tom began experimenting

Victor Appleton

with various circuit designs. He worked through the afternoon and returned to the problem early the next morning.

He was interrupted by a message from Art Wiltessa, reporting no luck so far in finding the missile. Later, shortly before lunch, Tom received another call, this time from Admiral Walter. "Just wanted to keep you posted, Tom. Our task force reports no success on their part in finding the buried missile. No sign of the enemy, either."

"They'd probably hesitate to attack any official U.S. Navy units," Tom said. "Or it might mean they've already found the missile themselves."

"That's what I fear," Admiral Walter confessed gloomily. "However, we'll continue searching."

Tom promised to fly down to the site at the first opportunity, saying he was developing a new device that might assist in the search. After snatching a hasty lunch, Tom returned to work.

Arv Hanson machined several parts and molded the plastic face mask to Tom's specifications. By evening the new device was completed.

"Now for a test," the young inventor said to himself.

Sandy Swift and Phyl Newton were eager to watch the test, so the next morning they drove to the plant in Phyl's white convertible. Tom, clad in swim trunks, was waiting for them with Chow near the edge of a mammoth concrete tank. Set in bedrock, at one end of the Enterprises grounds, the tank was used for submarine testing.

When Sandy saw the power unit strapped to Tom's weight belt, she exclaimed, "*That* little gadget will supply all the air you need? Why, it's no bigger than a pocket transistor radio!"

Tom grinned. "I hope it will. That's what I intend to find out."

"How does it work?" Phyl asked, fascinated.

Tom explained, "Actually its function is to replace the carbon dioxide that I exhale with fresh oxygen drawn from the water. Otherwise, although the carbon dioxide I'd breathe out would be a very small amount at a time, it soon would make the air unfit. The nitrogen, which makes up much of the air we breathe, is chemically inert and can be used again and again."

He pointed to a round screen on one side of the unit. "This is the water intake," Tom went on, "and this other screen is where the water comes out after we've removed its oxygen."

Near the forward end of the unit, a semirigid plastic tube was connected, leading up to the face mask. At the rear was a power port for inserting a small solar battery.

"What about this little tuning knob?" Sandy asked.

"That's the rate control for adjusting the output frequency to the wearer's breathing rate." Tom added, "I've decided to call the whole apparatus an 'electronic hydrolung.'"

Chow pushed back his ten-gallon hat and scratched his head dubiously. "Wal, I'm keepin' a net handy to drag you out, boss, just in case."

Tom chuckled and fitted the mask over his face, then made a clean dive into the tank. For the next ten minutes the girls and Chow watched wide-eyed as he swam, walked around, and went through vigorous exercises at the bottom of the tank without once coming up for air.

"Whee!" Sandy exclaimed when Tom finally climbed out. "Make me one, so I can take up skin diving!"

"It's wonderful!" Phyl added admiringly.

Tom took off his mask. "I'm pretty pleased with it myself," he admitted, grinning.

The girls stayed at Enterprises for lunch. Then the group, accompanied by Doc Simpson, flew to Fearing Island so Tom could test his invention in deep water. Boarding a small motor launch, with Doc at the helm, they cruised out to a suitable depth and dropped anchor.

"Don't become too confident, Tom," Doc warned. "I'll drop a signal line over the side in case of emergency."

Tom buckled on his equipment belt and adjusted the face mask. Then he held up crossed fingers and back-flipped over the gunwale into the water. Chow, Doc, and the girls watched his plummeting figure fade from view.

Tom, an expert skin diver, had never before felt such a sense of ease and freedom under water. He was moving, light and self-contained, in a green, magical world. With no air tanks chafing his back, he felt akin to the fishes themselves.

"Wish I'd brought a hook and line along." He chuckled, as a school of mackerel darted past.

Now came the real test. Deeper and deeper, Tom cleaved his way downward. Reaching bottom, he prowled about the ocean bed for a while, then started up again. Suddenly a stab of pain shot through his chest - a warning of nitrogen bubbles forming in his blood!

Tom swam toward the signal cord, dangling dimly in the distance. By the time he reached it, his muscles were knotting with cramps.

"It's the bends again, all right!" Tom realized. Gritting his teeth, he yanked hard on the line, then summoned his strength to hang on.

Doc and Chow hauled up frantically. Tom's face was contorted with pain when they finally got him aboard and stripped off his mask.

"Oh! How awful!" Phyl gasped.

Sandy cradled Tom's head in her lap, and Phyl held his hand sympathetically, while Doc Simpson injected a hypodermic to ease the pain. Chow steered the launch back to shore, and Tom was rushed to the base infirmary in an ambulance.

Here he was placed in a decompression chamber for several hours and later transferred to a hospital bed. Bud Barclay came to visit him.

"We're a fine couple of fish," he said.

Tom chuckled wryly. "*Live* fish, anyhow."

"In my case, thanks to you," Bud said.

"Forget it, pal. The score's about even, I should think," Tom said, recalling the many life-or-death adventures they had shared.

Bud was thrilled to hear of Tom's electronic hydrolung. The young inventor spent the evening sketching out an improved design to eliminate future accidents.

"I'll install a special device to remove the nitrogen as the wearer exhales," Tom explained. "Then a valve will feed in helium to replace it. Since helium doesn't dissolve in the blood like nitrogen does, it will not bubble out when the pressure is reduced. Should have thought of that before!"

"But you'll need a tank for the helium, won't you?" Bud objected.

Tom shook his head. "Enough can be compressed into a small capsule to supply the wearer's needs. Remember, it can be used over and over again."

"Pretty neat," Bud commented.

By morning Tom felt thoroughly recovered. He insisted upon flying back to Enterprises to make the necessary changes in his hydrolung. Bud accompanied him, eager to get back on the job.

In a few hours Tom had added a small fitting to his power unit to provide for helium substitution. Then the two boys hopped back to Fearing for a second deep-water test. This time, Tom was delighted to find that he could operate comfortably at great depths, as well as rise or descend suddenly without ill effect.

Bud was aglow with enthusiasm. "Boy, we can really explore now!"

After the boys had returned to Enterprises, Tom phoned Arv Hanson and asked that a duplicate of the hydrolung be turned out in the shop as soon as possible. It was ready the following Monday morning, so Tom suggested to his father that the two visit the proposed underwater site and make some sample plantings.

"Great idea, son," Mr. Swift agreed. "I want to try out your new diving apparatus myself. If it's successful, we'll be able to tackle two problems at once - recover the Jupiter prober and start the 'sea farm.'"

They flew to Fearing, then went by boat to the farm site, about half a mile offshore. Each carried several of the valuable Far Eastern plants.

The silt beds which Mr. Swift had selected were just deep enough to keep the plants from being discovered, yet enable them to receive sufficient sunlight.

Tom and his father started their planting. But no sooner had the first plants been embedded than fish darted in to nibble them. Even the roots disappeared into their greedy maws.

"Looks as though we'll have to build some sort of net enclosure around and over our farm," Mr. Swift said, after they had climbed back into the boat. "But at least your hydrolung device is a great success, son!"

Tom was thoughtful. "Dad, I wonder if the fish would eat those plants from space which you've been growing under salt water?"

Tom was referring to certain strange plants rocketed to earth by unknown space friends with whom the Swifts had been in communication.

"I have a hunch," Tom went on, "that the fish might be repelled by the unusual scent of those space plants. If so, we could scatter them among the earth plants to keep the fish away."

Mr. Swift was impressed by Tom's idea. As soon as they had returned to Enterprises, he proposed that the experiment get under way.

Tom volunteered to undertake the job at once with Bud. While the young inventor phoned his copilot, Mr. Swift went to his own laboratory to prepare the plants for shipment.

Twenty minutes later the boys took off in a jet. The plants had been parceled in transparent plastic film. Glistening with a red metallic sheen, they looked somewhat like tulips with honeycombed centers.

"Scarecrow plants to drive off fishes," Bud joked. "What will scientists think of next!"

Tom laughed, then abruptly frowned. "Hey! What's that character up to?" he said. "Trying to buzz us?"

A sleek gray jet without markings was arrowing in on them from three o'clock. Bud flicked on the radio and barked a warning. The plane made no response. As it kept coming, Tom increased speed - then rolled, dived, and changed course, but failed to shake off their pursuer.

Bud, meanwhile, was frantically calling Enterprises and a nearby airport, but getting no response. Yet their radio was working, for a voice suddenly crackled:

"Follow the mystery plane for a landing and you won't be harmed!"

CHAPTER V

A HUNCH PAYS OFF

Dismayed, Tom and Bud stared at each other. Apparently the enemy ship had blanked out their radio communication to all points except the mystery plane.

"Who are you and what do you want?" Tom said into his microphone.

The voice replied crisply, "*You'll find out when the time comes!*"

Tom flicked off his mike and exchanged another worried glance with Bud. "We seem to be in a spot, pal!"

"And how! Especially if that crate's armed!" Bud muttered. "But what are they after?"

Tom shrugged. "The space plants maybe - or possibly our jet."

"Might even be *us* they want," Bud said. "Got any tricks under your magician's hat?"

Tom's brain was already racing to figure a way out. Suddenly he snapped his fingers. "Hey! I almost forgot!" he exclaimed. "Look in the locker, Bud, and see if we have the radio set that neutralizes all interference!"

Bud's face brightened. "Now you're talking!"

Victor Appleton

The set had been perfected during Tom's *Cosmic Astronauts* adventure, in defense against an Oriental enemy's jamming-wave generator. Bud found it in the locker, dragged it out joyfully, and plugged it into the power supply.

Meanwhile, the mystery jet had banked in a wide circle and headed west. As Tom stalled for time, it swooped back again and the same voice came snarling over the speaker.

"I warned you to follow us! Or would you prefer to be shot down?"

As if to back up the threat, a burst of tracer fire grazed Tom's plane.

He hastily switched on his mike. "Okay, hold your fire! I guess we have no choice!"

The jet turned back on its westerly course, and Tom followed obediently. Meanwhile, Bud had warmed up the other radio and contacted Enterprises. Tom switched mikes long enough to report their position, course, and speed, adding:

"Tell Security to alert Vignall Air Force Base pronto!"

"Roger Wilco!" the Enterprises operator responded. Even if the enemy ship detected the call, Tom knew the automatic scrambling device would prevent the message from being understood.

Minute after minute, the flight continued. "Where are they taking us?" Bud muttered.

"Some out-of-the-way landing spot probably," Tom conjectured. "I wonder how soon those fighter boys will -"

Bud suddenly grabbed Tom's arm and pointed to starboard. "There they come, skipper!"

Three gleaming specks had just burst through a cloud bank to the north. Closing in rapidly, they were soon visible as Air Force fighter jets, flying in V formation.

"Fighter One to unmarked jet!" came the sharp command over the radio. "Can you read me?... You'd *better* read me, pal! I order you to proceed to Vignall Air Base under our escort or take the consequences!"

The mystery pilot, evidently bewildered by the sudden onslaught, made a frantic effort to escape. But the fighters, with almost contemptuous ease, quickly surrounded the plane and forced him to comply with orders.

Bud whooped with laughter. "Just a sheep in wolf's clothing, eh, buster?"

Minutes later, all the planes, including Tom's, landed at the airfield. Four sullen-faced men, their hands up, emerged from the mystery jet. Military police with drawn automatics herded them to the commandant's office. Tom and Bud followed.

"Attempted aerial piracy, eh?" the commandant said when he heard the boys' story. Turning to the prisoners, he snapped, "Who are you, and what's the meaning of all this?"

The crew captain, a hard-looking, stockily built man of about forty-five, rasped back, "We have nothing to say."

The commandant wasted no words. "Search them," he told the MP's.

Their wallets and various other items revealed little. The crew captain was carrying a private pilot's license on which he was identified as "Jack Smith." The names of the others, as shown on identification papers of one kind or another, sounded equally false.

"Probably all forged," the commandant muttered, "but we'll check them out."

He tried again to glean something from the prisoners, but they replied with sneering evasions. The commandant reddened with anger at their stubbornness. "All right. Take them to the guardhouse," he ordered.

As the MP's marched the hijackers off, Tom asked how their case would be handled.

"The crime is a federal offense," the commandant explained. "Air Force Intelligence will co-operate on the case, but the prisoners will be turned over to a federal marshal."

Tom briefed him on the background of the situation, including the Jupiter-probing missile mystery, then asked, "Could those men be transferred to the Shopton jail for the time being so our own security setup can take a hand in the investigation?"

The commandant nodded. "I'll arrange it."

As the boys flew back to Enterprises, Bud threw Tom a quizzical glance. "How come you mentioned the Jupiter prober, skipper? Do you think those hijackers were after information?"

Tom shrugged. "I'm wondering myself, Bud. If they were, it could mean our enemy hasn't found it yet!"

When they arrived at the experimental station, Tom made a full report to Harlan Ames, the slim, dark-haired security chief. Ames listened thoughtfully but was as baffled as Tom.

"Are the men Americans?" he asked.

"I doubt it," Tom said. "They speak English well enough, but with a faint accent. Somehow, I have a hunch they're Brungarians."

Ames whistled. "That could spell trouble, skipper." More than once, Brungarian rebel agents had engaged in brazen plots against America and the Swifts.

"Let's hope I'm wrong," Tom said wryly.

"Art Wiltessa - and the Navy - called again," Ames added. "Still no luck on the missile search."

The gloomy news did nothing to lift Tom's spirits. The next day, hoping to verify or disprove his suspicion, he drove to Shopton Police Headquarters with Harlan Ames. The two talked briefly with Chief Slater, an old friend. Then a turnkey took them to the cell block.

The four prisoners had been confined in a single large cell. They seemed tense and angry - as if they had been quarreling among themselves.

"Ready to talk yet?" Ames asked. Getting no reply, he repeated the question in Brungarian.

Ames's ruse failed. "What language is that?" asked "Captain Smith" mockingly. "Pig Latin?"

As his cellmates grinned, Tom's eyes roved over their faces. One man - wavy-haired with penetrating dark eyes - seemed oddly familiar. Why? Suddenly the answer hit Tom like a flash. He resembled Streffan Mirov, the brilliant Brungarian rocket scientist who had tried to oust Tom's expedition from the phantom satellite Nestria.

Playing a hunch, Tom said to him, "You know what your government does to rebels and bunglers, Mirov."

The man stiffened and paled. "We have not b-b-bungled!" he stuttered angrily.

"Shut up, you fool!" their leader shouted.

Victor Appleton

CHAPTER VI

THE CAISSON CLUE

"Captain Smith" had leaped to his feet, quivering with anger. But it was too late. His cellmate, by answering to the name of "Mirov," had given away their nationality!

Tom and Ames exchanged grins of triumph.

"No doubt you recall what happened to Streffan Mirov," Tom went on, pressing his advantage. "Or should I say the *late* Streffan Mirov? Our last report was that he had been tried and condemned by your own government. Perhaps you can give us news of his fate?"

The wavy-haired prisoner's eyes blazed with hate. "Grin while you can, Tom Swift! Because of you, my brother Streffan is now serving a long prison sentence! But I, Dimitri Mirov, will get revenge!"

"You blame Tom Swift because your brother botched his job of claiming the satellite Nestria by force and fraud?" Ames taunted.

"Our space friends moved that asteroid into orbit around the earth," Tom added. "We claimed it by right of first landing. Even your own leaders couldn't agree to Streffan's crazy scheme to destroy everything."

Dimitri Mirov lost all control and burst into a volley of guttural Brungarian abuse.

"I warn you, Swift!" he choked. "Jailing us will not make you safe - or your projects, either!"

A blow to the head from "Captain Smith" sent Mirov reeling back against the wall. "Fool! Maybe that will quiet you!" the pilot snapped viciously. "You have said too much already!"

"Let's go, Tom," said Ames. "We've learned the information we came for."

The prisoners could only glare in baffled rage through the cell bars as Tom and the security chief turned their backs and walked away.

"Nice going, Tom," Ames murmured. "Your hunch certainly paid off." Chief Slater added his congratulations when he heard how Tom had trapped Mirov into disclosing his identity.

Both Tom and Ames were grave as they drove back to the plant. Neither took Mirov's threats lightly.

Tom pondered another angle. Were the Brungarian rebels perhaps responsible for the attempted theft of the Jupiter-circling missile?

Ames was inclined to think so. "Moreover," he forecast, "it's a cinch they haven't thrown their last punch. I'll pass the word to the FBI and Central Intelligence."

After lunch Tom flew to Fearing Island with Bud, eager to tackle their interrupted job of rooting the space plants into the undersea silt beds. Zimby Cox, a sandy-haired, freckle-faced jetmariner, volunteered to pilot a motor launch for them.

They sped across the water, then dropped anchor at the farm

Victor Appleton

site. Tom and Bud donned their hydrolung gear and went over the side, each clutching containers of the space plants.

Reaching bottom, they glided about in the shadowy green water, embedding the plants at far-spaced intervals. The Tomasite-producing plants had been almost completely devoured. A few fish were darting about, but they swam off quickly at the boys' approach. To Tom's delight, they showed no sign of returning.

"Looks as if our keep-off signs are working," Tom said with a pleased chuckle when the boys finally surfaced and climbed back aboard the boat.

Bud nodded. "Smart idea, all right." Then he scowled thoughtfully. "But if you ask me, skipper, fishes aren't the only thieves you'll have to guard against."

"Meaning?"

"Mirov's pals," Bud replied. "If it's the space plants they were after when they pulled that aerial hijack attempt, they could take them easily from these silt beds."

Tom sobered. "You have a point there. I'd better have an audio screen set up around this whole area. That'll act as a burglar alarm - and help discourage the fish, too."

Twenty minutes later the boys were winging back to the mainland. When Tom reached his office, he called in Gib Brownell, an Enterprises engineer.

"Got a job for me, skipper?"

Tom handed him a hastily scribbled diagram of the audio-screen setup. "One of those hurry-up deals, Gib," he said with an apologetic grin. Tom explained his plan. "We'll use transmitter buoys, monitored by an alarm system at base headquarters on Fearing."

Brownell studied the diagram and nodded. "Right. We can have it set up in twenty-four hours."

As Brownell left the office, the telephone jangled. Tom reached for it.

"Admiral Walter calling." His voice was tense. "Important news, Tom. One of our subs has picked up a clue that someone has been operating in the missile search area."

"What sort of clue, sir?" Tom asked.

"A compressed-air caisson for underwater work. It had been driven into the silt and then abandoned." Admiral Walter added that photographs and a section of the caisson were being flown to the Naval Research Laboratory for careful study. "I'll have a full report transmitted to you by video as soon as it reaches my desk."

Tom thanked the admiral and hung up, feeling more uneasy than ever. The report came through the following morning. Tom absorbed the contents, then gave a low whistle.

"Trouble?" asked Bud, who had just dropped into the office with some flight-test data on a new Swift superjet.

"Our old enemies again." Tom shoved the papers across his desk.

The report stated that both the design and manufacturing techniques used in making the caisson indicated that it was of Brungarian origin. A spectrographic analysis of the steels confirmed the theory. Their metallurgical content agreed with known Brungarian steel formulas.

"The sneaky rats!" Bud cried out. "Well, at least we know now who sabotaged our missile recovery."

As Tom paced about the office, Bud added, "What do you

Victor Appleton

suppose they were using the caisson for?"

"Probably as a base for some heavy, rotating search equipment," the young inventor surmised.

"But why ditch it?"

Tom shrugged. "An optimistic guess is that they spotted our Navy search force and pulled out quickly, fearing a surprise attack."

"What's a pessimistic explanation?" Bud asked.

"Mission completed," Tom said grimly. "No need for them to stick around if they'd already snagged the missile."

Bud scowled at the thought. "Oh, no! That mustn't be true!"

Tom plopped down at his desk, frowning. "Bud, I've been itching to get to work on a non-detectable sub, like the one that attacked us. But maybe it would be smarter to get a line on Mirov's pals first."

"You mean down in the South Atlantic?"

Tom nodded. "I'd sure like to know if they found that missile."

"You and I both, pal!" Bud agreed. "Hey! We could use the electronic hydrolungs for scouting around!" he added eagerly.

"I intend to," Tom said. "But we'll need speed to cover the area. So first I want to add an ion drive to our equipment."

"Ion drive? For underwater?" Bud, who was familiar with ion propulsion for spaceships, wrinkled his brow in a puzzled frown.

"A goofy idea just occurred to me, but I think it may work

out," Tom replied. He seized a pencil and began explaining what he had in mind.

The drive unit would take water into itself, separate the ionized molecules, and expose them to an electric field. Thus a stream of water would be forced out. This procedure, in turn, would set up a siphoning action through a central tube - in effect, creating a small but powerful water-jet motor.

"We'll be human submarines!" Bud exclaimed.

By the time Bud left the laboratory half an hour later, Tom had already plunged into work on his newest invention. The idea was simple enough in itself, Tom felt. The main problem would be the design job - laying out a compact, lightweight unit which a swimmer could easily carry on his back.

Fascinated, the young inventor worked late into the evening, stopping only in response to a telephone plea from Mrs. Swift. By midmorning the next day, Tom had assembled a pilot model of his ion-drive jet. In appearance, it was a slender metal cylinder, two feet long, with an inner concentric tube projecting at each end.

Tom had ordered a tank set up in his laboratory to test the unit. The tank was filled chest-deep with water, and the ion drive was mounted on a unitrack running the length of it. Tom set up his control board alongside, with the main power switch within easy reach. The drive unit was connected to the board by a suspended cable.

"Boy, this'll be like playing with a speedboat in a bathtub!" Tom thought with a chuckle as he changed into swim trunks.

He climbed into the tank and slid the drive unit to one end of its track. Then Tom metered out power slowly. With a gentle *whoosh*, the ion-drive unit whizzed along the unitrack to the other end of the tank.

"Not bad," Tom muttered, a pleased grin on his face. "Now I'll rev it up a little."

He slid the drive unit back to starting position, then opened the switch wider. He had just started across the tank himself when suddenly he became powerless to move.

Tom was pinned helplessly against the wall of the tank by the powerful water-jet exhaust! And the control switch was beyond his reach!

CHAPTER VII

PORPOISE TAG

"Good grief! I'm trapped!" Tom squirmed desperately in a vain attempt to free himself.

The ion-drive unit had hurtled to the far end of the tank at the first flick of power. But its exhaust tube was still jetting out a current of water with stunning force. Tom could feel the near-crushing pressure against his chest, even the full length of the tank away!

"H-h-help!" Tom gasped.

Moments dragged by with agonizing slowness. Tom felt as if his last ounce of breath were being squeezed out by the viselike pressure.

Suddenly a gravelly Western voice reached him, singing "Home on the Range." It drew closer, swelling into a foghorn drone as the lab door swung open.

"Good old Chow!" Tom thought. "Thank heavens!"

The grizzled, bowlegged cook ambled cheerfully into the laboratory, pushing a lunch cart. But, to Tom's dismay, he cast only a passing glance at the figure in the tank.

"Soup's on, son!" Chow announced loudly. He began to ladle

Victor Appleton

out a bowl of oyster stew from a steaming pot. Evidently he had not realized the young inventor's dilemma!

"Extra good today too, if I do say so myself!" the old Texan went on, setting out the rest of the lunch. "Well, come on, buckaroo! Break away from them chores an' dive in! Brand my cactus salad, if there's one thing that riles a cook -"

Summoning all his strength, Tom croaked out weakly, "Chow!... Get help!"

At the strange sound of Tom's voice, Chow jerked around. His eyes bugged out at the look on the young inventor's face. Then he dashed to the public-address outlet on the wall and switched on the mike.

"Help! Help!" Chow yelled. "Tom Jr.'s trapped in his lab!"

The roly-poly chef was quivering in panic. He dashed across the room and paced helplessly about the tank. Within moments, excited men were crowding into the laboratory.

Mr. Swift, among the first to arrive, took in the situation at a glance. He dashed to the control board and slammed shut the main switch, thus cutting off power to the ion-drive jet.

"Whew! Th-thanks, Dad!" Tom's chest was heaving as he gulped in air to relieve his tortured lungs.

Tom Sr. helped him climb out of the tank.

"B-b-brand my rhubarb rockets," Chow stuttered. "What in tarnation happened?"

"Guess I gunned my new skin-diving jet a bit too hard," Tom said sheepishly. "It was almost a K.O. for me!"

Mr. Swift asked Tom about the invention. After explaining how it worked, Tom added with a grin, "Maybe you'd better hang around, Dad, until I install some sort of density-control gadget for my hydrolung. Then I can go up or down, or stay at any level easily."

Such a device, Tom felt, might prove to be a lifesaver if he should ever become trapped under water - perhaps far from help.

The elder scientist chuckled and threw an arm around Tom's shoulders. "I'd say you could design something like that with your eyes shut, son!"

Warmed by his father's appreciation, Tom set to work improving his diving apparatus.

An hour later Bud came bursting into the laboratory. "Hey! What's this I hear about your getting hammerlocked by a water jet?" the husky young pilot asked. He had been on a test flight and just returned.

Tom laughed good-naturedly. "Nothing serious. In fact, I felt pretty silly," he told his chum. "I souped up our ion-drive gizmo a bit too much."

Bud picked up the slender metal cylindrical assembly from the workbench. "This it?" he asked, his curiosity immediately aroused.

Tom nodded and demonstrated the device in the test tank.

Bud whistled with glee. "Boy! With this rig, we can scoot around like a pair of barracudas!" he exclaimed. "What about that other thing you're working on?" Bud pointed to a small electronic chassis on the workbench, studded with a tangle of transistors, diodes, and condensers.

"It's a density-control device," Tom explained. "A substitute for ballast tanks, you might say. It'll enable us to rise or sink to any depth at will, simply by varying our underwater density."

Tom said the device would be carried in a small case, hooked to the diver's belt, with a single tuning-knob control. The "throttle" or speed control for the ion drive would be housed in the same unit.

"I can't wait to try out the new diving gear," Bud said excitedly.

By four o'clock Tom had the apparatus perfected, and turned it over to Arv Hanson for fast duplication.

"We'll give it a shakedown tomorrow morning," he told Bud.

The duplicates of the ion drive and density control were ready and waiting when the boys arrived at the plant next day. They immediately flew to Fearing Island and embarked in a motor launch, with Zimby Cox again at the helm.

This time they cruised out to deeper water. Tom and Bud donned flippers and belt, and helped each other strap on his ion-drive jet.

"*Down* we go, into the wilds of sharks!" Bud chortled lustily. "Watch your step, Tom."

"Just make sure you come up again in one piece," Zimby said with a grin. "Also, don't get carried away with that ion squirt gun and take off on a round-the-world underwater cruise."

"Who knows?" Tom joked. Adjusting his face mask, he plunged over the side. Bud followed.

Down they glided into the sea-green wilderness. Leveling off in sight of the ocean floor, they tried their drive jets. The effect was thrilling! *Zip ... Whoosh!* They darted to and fro like human torpedoes.

Then Tom twirled the control knob of his density unit. Immediately he bobbed upward like a cork. A reverse twirl sent him plummeting toward the bottom again. Bud, watching with wide-eyed excitement, began experimenting on his own.

Soon the boys were engaging in all sorts of underwater acrobatics. Presently Bud felt a nudge in the back that sent him hurtling a dozen yards through the water.

"Snuck up on me, eh, pal?" he thought with a chuckle. "Okay, Tom old boy, here's where the undersea terror strikes back!"

Swooping around to return the compliment, Bud gulped in surprise. Instead of his chum, he found himself face to face with a bottle-nosed dolphin!

"Good night!" Bud thought. "A porpoise! So you're the joker who nudged me!"

With a playful toss of its comical-looking snout, the porpoise swam off, as if inviting Bud to join in the fun and games. A whole school of the creatures cavorted into view.

"Okay! If you want to play!" Chuckling, Bud darted in pursuit, whacked the porpoise that had nudged him, and jetted off again. The porpoise gave chase, whistling and grunting audibly.

Tom joined in the fun, and soon a rollicking game of under-water tag was in full swing. The dolphins seemed as playful and mischievous as small children.

Twenty minutes later the boys surfaced and hauled themselves aboard. Both tore off their masks and flopped into the boat, shaking with laughter, surfacing and diving.

"What was so funny down there?" Zimby asked.

When Tom told him about the dolphins, he too burst into laughter. The porpoises rose into view and convoyed the launch all the way back to the island.

Victor Appleton

The boys were so jubilant over the performance of the new hydrolung gear that Tom decided to press his search for the Brungarian sea-prowlers immediately. Soon after lunch they took off in the *Sea Hound* and headed for the South Atlantic. Hank Sterling, Chow Winkler, and two crewmen accompanied the boys.

Dazzling afternoon sunshine sparkled over the sea when they reached the missile search area. Tom immediately contacted Art Wiltessa and the task-force ships. They had no new developments to report.

The young inventor gave orders to submerge. As soon as the seacopter touched bottom, Tom and Bud swam out through the air lock with their hydrolungs.

They probed about for half an hour, ranging farther and farther from the *Sea Hound*. Then Tom felt a touch on his arm. He turned and saw Bud pointing off excitedly to the right.

A strange submarine was moving slowly toward them!

CHAPTER VIII

DATE TROUBLE

The boys exchanged looks of fear through their face masks as the knifelike hull and conning tower of the submarine loomed gray and ghostly.

Was the sub Brungarian? And what was it up to? Were the two young skin divers about to be run down or kidnaped?

Or was its crew friendly?

"Better not chance it," Tom decided fast. He caught Bud's eye again and motioned upward with a jerk of his thumb. "Topside, pal!"

"Roger!" Bud's lips shaped the word silently behind his face mask.

In a twinkling both boys flicked their density controls and zoomed upward. The sub at once seemed to betray a hostile intent. It blew its tanks and planed upward in pursuit. But Tom and Bud easily pulled away. Their density units worked like magic, shooting them straight toward the surface.

"Wow!" Bud shoved back his face mask as they broke water. "That baby was after us and no mistake!"

Tom nodded, treading water. "Let's not stick around here,

either! We'll soon have company again if we do!"

Bud did not argue. "Where to, skipper?"

In the fresh salt air, with the sunshine sparkling on the waves, it was hard to believe that an enemy submarine was hot on their trail. But both youths realized their peril was growing by the moment.

"Back toward the *Sea Hound*," Tom said, pointing north-northwest. "Submerge as we go!"

Bud circled his thumb and forefinger, then adjusted his mask, and the two boys plunged back in. On a sloping downward course, they sped along like undersea rockets, their ion jets functioning perfectly. Minutes later, they sighted the seacopter.

Hank waved to them through the cabin window as they glided past. The air lock opened speedily and the two boys entered. Both heaved sighs of relief when they were safely inside.

"Somethin' wrong?" Chow asked, sniffing trouble.

"A strange submarine," Tom reported. "Brungarian more than likely. It may be heading this way if they've tracked us."

"A sub?" Hank was startled. "We've picked up nothing on sonar!"

"Check again," Tom ordered.

The sonarman bent to his scope and Hank listened intently over the hydrophones. Neither could detect any sign of another craft.

"Probably the same one that fired on us the last time," Tom said grimly. "We'd better clear out before they take another pot shot at us."

Hank sent the *Sea Hound* zooming toward the surface while the boys changed quickly into slacks and T shirts. Then Tom took over the controls for the flight home.

"Brand my vitamin vittles! Are we just goin' to turn tail an' run every time them varmints come skulkin' around?" Chow fumed as the seacopter arrowed northward.

"Not if I can help it," Tom vowed. "But first I must figure out a way to make our own craft invisible, so to speak. It's the only way to protect our American crews, Chow, if we hope to do any secret digging for that lost missile."

"Want another suggestion, skipper?" Bud put in. "This one is about the hydrolung."

"Sure. Speak up."

"How about putting some sort of communications system into our hydrolung gear? If I hadn't been close enough to grab you when I spotted that sub, it might have been curtains, pal!"

"You're right," Tom agreed. "I'll get to work on it."

It was sunset when Fearing Island came into sight. The boys flew a Pigeon Special back to Enterprises, where Tom phoned a full report on the mystery sub to the Navy Department. Then the two chums drove to the Swift home for a late supper.

Phyl Newton was visiting Sandy that evening, but the girls displayed a marked coolness toward Tom and Bud. Instead of engaging in conversation, they retired to Sandy's room upstairs to play records, while Mrs. Swift served the boys a warmed-up but tasty meal of roast beef and mince pie.

"What's wrong? Are we repulsive or something?" Bud asked as they ate.

Tom shrugged, concentrating on a mouthful of roast beef.

"Search me. We sure don't seem very popular with the girls tonight."

Mrs. Swift, overhearing their remarks in the kitchen, smiled but maintained a diplomatic silence.

Suddenly Bud slapped his forehead. "Good night! No wonder!"

Tom looked up with a grin of interest. "Well, what have we done?"

"It's what we *haven't* done, pal!" Bud retorted. "We had a date this afternoon, remember? That beach party and dance put on by Sandy and Phyl's school sorority!"

Tom gulped. "Oops! Boy, we really did pull a boner this time! I completely forgot!"

As they finished supper, the boys discussed various ways to make amends. Boxes of chocolates? Flowers? None of their ideas seemed to have the proper spark.

"We'll have to come up with something super," Bud said.

"Right!" Tom agreed. "Let's sleep on it and see if we can't dream up something by tomorrow morning that'll really wow them."

The next morning Tom had a flash of inspiration as he drove to the plant in his sports car. He hailed Bud at the first opportunity.

"I have it, pal! What say we stage an old-fashioned square dance Tuesday night at the yacht club on Lake Carlopa?"

Bud's eyes lighted up. "Hey, that's a great idea! We'll invite a whole gang, get Chow to handle the refreshments, and make it a real shindig!"

The boys shook hands enthusiastically. Eager to patch matters up as soon as possible, they invited Sandy and Phyl out to lunch that day. Over dessert, the boys announced their plans for a square dance.

"We - uh - realize we goofed yesterday on that beach party," Tom said sheepishly. "But we're hoping you'll give us another chance."

The girls looked at each other, their eyes twinkling, then burst into giggles.

"You're forgiven completely!" Phyl declared.

"Then it's a date?" Bud put in.

"You bet it's a date, and don't you forget it!" Sandy warned. "Phyl and I are going right over to Dorman's Department Store and pick out some cute outfits for the dance!"

Tom and Bud chuckled over the success of their scheme as they drove back to Enterprises. Later that afternoon a telephone call interrupted Tom as he worked in his lab on a sonic-communications system for the hydrolung apparatus.

"This is Lester Morris," said the voice at the other end of the line. The name did not register with Tom at first until his caller added, "I hear you're planning a square dance Tuesday night at the yacht club."

Suddenly Tom remembered. Lester Morris was a popular dance orchestra leader in and around Shopton. He was also much in demand as a square-dance caller and fiddler.

"That's right," Tom said with a chuckle. "News must travel fast. We just phoned invitations to our friends."

Morris asked if musicians had been hired for the evening. When Tom said No, his caller volunteered for the job, offering to provide a small combo of country-style players. His asking price sounded like a bargain rate, and Tom, knowing Morris's reputation, was only too glad to engage him.

"Lucky break, his calling," the young inventor thought as he hung up.

Bud was delighted to hear of the arrangement when he came into the laboratory a while later. The boys talked over their dance plans for a few moments, then Bud asked:

"How's our underwater talkie system coming?"

Tom scratched his jaw thoughtfully. "A bit tricky but not too difficult," he replied. "It's mostly a job of adapting the sonar-phone arrangement from our Fat Man suits - in miniature."

A tiny mike, Tom explained, would be installed on the inside of each face mask, with its output feeding to a sonar transducer on the exterior. The receiving transducers would feed from amplifiers to earphones. The hookup would be powered by the solar battery in the hydrolung power unit, by connecting wires through the breathing tube.

"That's neat, Tom," Bud said. "Need any help?"

"You can mold us a pair of new face masks - big enough to cover the earphones," Tom suggested. He handed Bud a penciled sketch from the workbench, adding, "Then drill the holes for the mikes and earphones - the dimensions are there on the drawing. But watch it so you don't crack the plastic."

While Bud complied, Tom began assembling the tiny electronic parts. In two hours the gear was ready for testing.

Tom wiped his perspiring forehead and gave Bud a grin of satisfaction. "Go get your swim trunks, fly boy. Let's give it a tryout in the tank."

"Swell idea! Be back in a jiff!"

After a quick change, the boys strapped on the new hydrolung equipment. Before adjusting his face mask, Tom mentioned that he had inserted scrambling circuits into the communicators to foil any enemy eavesdroppers.

"If they do pick up anything, it'll sound like chop suey," Tom ended with a chuckle.

The boys submerged in the test tank and proceeded to give the new underwater communication system a thorough check-out. It worked perfectly. Ten minutes later Tom and Bud clambered out again, dripping wet but well satisfied.

They had just peeled off their masks when Chow came charging into the lab, with a crowd of workmen and technicians at his heels. The cook was wild-eyed with panic.

"What's wrong, Chow?" Tom asked in alarm.

CHAPTER IX

A MAGNETIC KIDNAPING

"The space people or some enemy's invadin' us!" Chow shouted. "Take a squint through your telescope, boss! Brand my bazooka, they may be landin' any second!"

More people came streaming in, attracted by the chef's cries and gesticulations. Some were bewildered, a few frightened. Others were laughing, thinking the whole thing a joke. The scene was rapidly taking on the proportions of a riot!

"Whoa! Slow down, Chow!" Tom ordered, trying to make himself heard above the din.

"It - it's the truth, boss!" Chow stammered, mopping his brow with a huge red bandanna. "Why, sufferin' rattlesnakes, didn't I hear 'em spoutin' their space lingo with my own ears?"

"You heard *what*?" Bud said.

"Spoutin' space talk!" the cook repeated. "It come right over the loud-speaker in the galley! They was chitter-chatterin' plottin' to blow us all to smithereens!"

"That's a fact! We heard it, too!" one of the workmen chimed in.

Tom and Bud looked at each other blankly. Then suddenly

Tom's eyes kindled with a dawning suspicion. Whirling around, he rushed over to inspect the public-address outlet on the wall.

Meanwhile, Mr. Swift had just driven in through the main gate of Enterprises. "What's going on?" he asked the guard at the gate, noting the excited hubbub around Tom's laboratory.

"Don't rightly know, sir," the guard replied. "I was wondering myself. I know it sounds crazy, but I thought I heard someone yelling there was going to be a space attack."

Mr. Swift's eyebrows lifted in amazement. Without further discussion, he stepped on the accelerator and sped off along the paved drive. Seconds later, his car braked to a stop near Tom Jr.'s private laboratory. The scientist jumped out and made his way through the milling crowd.

"What's going on?" Mr. Swift stared in astonishment at Tom and Bud, who were both doubled up with laughter.

"A scrambled radio alert, Dad," Tom gasped between chuckles. "Chow thought some Martian monsters were invading us, and sort of pushed the panic button."

The Texan blushed as Tom explained what had happened. Realizing Chow's embarrassment, Tom tried to make his mistake sound understandable.

Apparently the power line to the ion-drive control board had somehow picked up the boys' scrambled conversation underwater. The signal had been transferred by inductance in the wall wiring and amplified over the public-address system.

"Our wall mike was on," Tom added, "and it probably picked up some of the sound waves from the tank. Anyhow," he concluded, slapping the cook affectionately on the back, "I'm sure glad we have a wide-awake hombre like Chow in the outfit. It wouldn't be the first time he's saved our necks!"

Victor Appleton

Chow perked up, and the employees, reassured, returned to their jobs.

"I have some news of my own," Mr. Swift announced with a smile as the room cleared. "But I'm afraid it'll sound pretty tame compared to a space attack."

"Let's hear it, Dad," Tom said eagerly.

"I've been conducting some experiments with those space plants," the elder scientist said. "It looks as though they may prove to be a valuable nutritional source."

The plants, Mr. Swift went on, showed promise of producing enormous amounts of protein quickly and cheaply - enough to increase the world's food supply by a sizable margin. Moreover, he had isolated a vitamin in this protein not found in any of man's present foods.

"Doc Simpson has been working with me," Mr. Swift concluded. "He has been doing some experiments of his own with a vitamin extract from the space plants. He thinks it may prove highly beneficial to human beings."

Tom was thrilled, and even Bud realized that Mr. Swift's cautious report could well turn out to be of history-making importance.

"I'd say your news makes a phony space attack look pretty tame, Dad," Tom said, his eyes flashing enthusiastically. "With the earth's population increasing, this could be the answer to the food problem."

"Don't tell Chow," Bud added, "or we may find spaceburgers on the next menu!"

The Swifts chuckled. Chow's hobby of concocting weird dishes was a standing joke at Enterprises, and already had led to such dubious triumphs as armadillo stew and rattlesnake soup.

Monday morning Tom buckled down seriously to the job of designing an undetectable sub. His drawing board was littered with sketches and diagrams when the phone rang, breaking in on his thoughts. Tom answered it with a scowl of impatience. The caller was Lester Morris.

"Could you meet me at the yacht club to talk over the dance program?" Morris asked.

Tom hesitated. For Sandy's and Phyl's sakes he was eager to do everything possible to make the square dance a success. But on the other hand....

"I'm pretty busy today," Tom said. "But my sister and my friend Bud Barclay can tell you what we want - probably better than I can. Suppose I ask them to meet you there after lunch?"

There was a slight pause. "Very well," Morris agreed, although he sounded a bit annoyed.

After hanging up, Tom phoned Bud and asked him to keep the appointment. Bud was only too happy to oblige, jumping at the chance to take Sandy out to lunch beforehand.

At one o'clock the husky young pilot and his date strolled into the yacht club lounge. Lester Morris was nowhere in sight, so they sat down to wait. Twenty minutes later the musician still had not appeared.

"I hope he hasn't forgotten," Sandy said, glancing at her wrist watch.

"If he's a square-dance caller, his memory ought to be extra good," Bud joked. "Fine thing if he can't even remember the time of day!"

After waiting a while longer, Bud decided to telephone

Morris's home. But at that moment a thin, seedy-looking man came into the lounge. His close-set eyes and loudly striped suit combined to give him a somewhat disreputable appearance.

"Good grief! Len Unger!" Sandy whispered. "What does he want with us?"

Unger was walking straight toward them. Both Bud and Sandy had met him occasionally around town and found him obnoxious.

"Sorry, but Morris got tied up," Unger informed them. "He sent me to talk to you."

Sandy's blue eyes met Bud's in a flicker of distaste, but she tried to conceal her feelings. "Please sit down," she invited Unger politely. "What square-dance numbers does Mr. Morris do?"

Len Unger shrugged. "You name 'em."

"But, my goodness," Sandy said, puzzled, "how do we know he'll have the squares I name?"

Unger stared at her as if he did not quite understand. "You mean, can he call off the dances you want? If he can't, I'll let you know."

"Does he do patter calls or singing calls?" Bud put in.

Again Unger hesitated, then said, "Both."

"Wonderful!" Sandy exclaimed gleefully. "I thought he only did singing calls." After a moment's thought, she went on, "Well, let's see. What about 'Birdie in the Cage'?... And 'The Gal from Arkansas' ... 'Uptown and Downtown'...."

Unger jotted the names on the back of an envelope. Pausing a moment, he remarked, "Guess your brother was too busy to make it today, eh, Miss Swift? What kind of ex-spearmints is he working on now?"

"I really couldn't say," Sandy replied coldly. She always made it a point not to discuss Tom Jr.'s or her father's research work with outsiders.

Unger persisted chattily, "I read where he handled that Jupiter probe shoot for the Navy."

"Let's get back to square dancing," snapped Bud. As he and Sandy finished planning the program, Len Unger continued to drop remarks and questions about "The Great Tom Swift" and his inventions. All prying queries were side-stepped.

As soon as possible Sandy and Bud cut short the conversation and left the yacht club. Unger's face wore an angry sneer as they walked out.

"What a creep!" Bud said, when he and Sandy were driving back in his red convertible.

Meanwhile, in his private laboratory at Enterprises, Tom was somewhat discouraged. He had tried several different experimental attacks on the problem of an undetectable submarine. None had worked out successfully.

"I thought that idea of a sonar-wave baffle might lead somewhere," he murmured, "but it looks as though I'm wrong."

Flopping down on a stool at his workbench, Tom cupped his chin in his hands. He was frowning, deep in thought, as the pudgy figure of Chow Winkler came into the laboratory.

"'Smatter, boss?" the cook inquired cheerfully. "Ain't your ole think box workin' today?"

"Doesn't seem to be," Tom confessed.

"Give it time, son. Tomorrow's another day," Chow said philosophically. "What you need is a haircut for the square dance."

Tom laughed in spite of himself. "Maybe you're right, Chow. Might help me think better."

Tom got off the stool and stretched out the kinks in his legs. He strolled outside with Chow, then scootered to the parking lot and hopped into his sleek, silver sports car.

A moment later he was whizzing off in the direction of Shopton. Nearing town, Tom turned off on a side-road short cut. He noticed in his mirror that a truck behind him also turned off.

"Really barreling along!" Tom thought. "If you're in such a hurry, the road's yours, pal."

He pulled over sharply, motioning the truck to pass. Instead, to Tom's surprise, it closed in straight behind him. The next moment, Tom saw a port open below the truck's hood and a strange-looking device pop out on a springlike steel cable.

It clamped magnetically to Tom's rear bumper! His car was caught like a fish on a line!

Tom stepped on the accelerator, trying to pull free. The truck at once swerved off the road, steering around a utility pole. As the cable tautened, there was a sickening screech of metal and the sports car was brought to a crashing halt!

Tom's head slammed against the side window. With a groan, the young inventor blacked out.

CHAPTER X

TELEPHONE CODE

As he regained consciousness, Tom's eyes fluttered open. Sparks of pain shot through his head. A groan escaped his lips.

"Oo-o! What hit me?" Tom wondered.

He was lying on a sofa in a strange room. Someone was seated nearby, watching him. Tom tried to move his limbs and sit up. Then he discovered that his wrists and ankles were tied with sash cord.

"Better lie still, sonny boy," a gruff voice advised. "You ain't goin' nowhere."

The man who had spoken got up from his chair and came over to the sofa. He was of medium height, very muscular looking, with cold, glittering eyes. Rolled-up shirt sleeves revealed his powerful, hairy arms.

"Where am I?" Tom asked, suddenly remembering the events on the road before he blacked out. "And what's this all about?"

The man said with a mirthless grin, "You're a prisoner. And you're goin' to stay here until the cops let Dimitri Mirov go. It's up to you how fast they spring him."

The huge man lifted a telephone from an end table adjoining

Victor Appleton

the sofa and set it on the floor alongside Tom.

"Here's a phone. Go ahead and use it, but don't try any funny stuff."

In spite of his headache, Tom's brain was racing. What to do now? He shut his eyes and screwed up his face in an expression of pain, pretending to be still groggy while he stalled for time to figure out his next move.

"How can *I* get Mirov out of jail?" Tom faltered.

"You figure it out!" the man snarled. "And you'd better get results if you want to stay healthy!"

Through half-slitted eyes, Tom noted the telephone number printed on the dial. Evidently his captor had not thought to remove it from the instrument. A lucky break!

If only, Tom thought, he could devise some way to transmit the number to Ames without arousing his captor's suspicion - the phone's location could then be traced!

What about some sort of double-talk code? For instance, Tom told himself, keep slipping numbers into the conversation in order to transmit the digits of the telephone number. Would Ames catch on?

The number shown was BArwick 3-7156. BA on the dial would be the same as "2, 2."

"Come on! Quit stalling!" the man said threateningly.

"How can I dial with my hands tied?" Tom objected.

"I'll do the dialing, wise guy!"

He lifted the phone from its cradle and extended it to his prisoner. Tom told him the Enterprises number, then asked for Ames's extension as the switchboard operator answered. A moment later the security chief's voice came over the line.

"Ames speaking."

"This is Tom Jr., Harlan." His captor bent close to the receiver as Tom replied, in order to overhear what was being said. "I've been thinking," the young inventor went on, "that it might be smart to have Mirov released."

"*Released!*" Ames gasped in surprise. "But why, skipper?"

"Well ... er ... as a good-will gesture," Tom said. "I think it might
prevent future trouble with the Brungarians, don't you?"

"I do not!" Ames exploded. "The idea sounds crazy!"

"I don't think it's *too* crazy or *too* risky," Tom argued. By emphasizing the words, he hoped to impress them on Ames's mind.

Tom's tone of voice and the farfetched nature of what he was saying had already triggered the security chief's suspicions. "Where are you calling from?" Ames asked after a tense pause.

"Shopton," Tom replied. "I just drove in for a haircut." With a chuckle, he added, "Haven't had one in *three* months. That's a whole *week* longer than I usually go!"

Would Ames understand that by "week" he meant *seven* days?... "*It's the best I can do*," Tom thought.

"Look, skipper, are you sure you want Mirov let out?" Ames said slowly. "I still think it's unwise."

"Consider it an order!" Tom snapped. "This is *one* thing I insist upon, Harlan. Shouldn't take more than *five* or *six* hours, should it, even if he has to wire the Brungarian Embassy

Victor Appleton

to put up bail?"

"It can probably be handled faster than that - if he has any friends around town," Ames said.

Tom took the cue. "Could be," he replied meaningfully.

Tom's captor snatched the phone away and slammed it back on the hook. "All right, smart boy! That's enough!" he growled, glaring at Tom.

Back at Enterprises, Ames hung up thoughtfully. Tom's reply to his last question about Mirov having "friends around town" had convinced Ames that the young inventor was a prisoner, speaking under duress. Moreover, it had seemed as if someone else's breathing was faintly audible in the background, close to the phone.

But what message had Tom tried to convey?

As a routine security-department precaution, Ames's phone was connected to a recorder which automatically taped all calls. Now, while he pondered the problem, Ames pressed a foot-treadle switch to play back the conversation.

Meanwhile, Tom and his captor waited tensely. From time to time the latter glanced at his watch. "Better hope that call does the trick, Swift," he muttered. "It's the only hope you got of leavin' here alive!"

"How will you know if they've turned Mirov loose?" Tom asked. He was wondering if he might persuade his captor to let him make a second call.

"Don't worry. Mirov knows how to contact me."

Half an hour dragged by - then forty minutes. Suddenly the door buzzer rang sharply. The man jerked to attention, obviously startled. He glanced at Tom, then toward the direction of the sound, moistening his lips nervously.

"He must have been expecting just a phone call," Tom decided.

The buzzer shrilled again. This time the man got up from his chair, gagged Tom hastily with a handkerchief, and went to the door.

"Who's there?" he asked loudly.

"Mirov! Let me in, Duffy!" replied an accented voice from outside.

With a look of relief, Duffy started to open the door - then froze as he saw not only Mirov, but two police officers and Ames accompanying him.

"Are you the one who's going to put up bail?" one of the officers demanded.

Duffy floundered, scenting danger but unable to pick up any clue from Mirov's face. "Why - uh - yeah, maybe. How much is it?"

"Ten million! Can you raise it?" Ames snapped sarcastically.

As Duffy gaped in confusion, the officers suddenly flung their weight forward. The door flew open and Duffy was thrown back, almost losing his balance. Beyond, through the small vestibule, Ames caught a glimpse of Tom on the sofa.

"There he is!" Ames shouted.

Moments later, Tom was untied. Mirov and Duffy were handcuffed together.

The young inventor shook hands joyfully with his rescuers. "Nice going,

Harlan! Boy, I was sweating icicles here, wondering if you'd be able to decipher all my double talk!"

"You made the numbers clear enough," the security chief said with a grin, "but it took a while to guess what they stood for. And then, of course, we had to trace the address through the telephone company."

Eying the ugly bruise on Tom's forehead, Ames added, "Sure you're all right?"

"Right now I feel swell!" Tom declared, chuckling. He told of his kidnaping, while one of the officers took down the details.

The prisoners were taken off to jail in the police squad car. Tom and Ames, meanwhile, in the security chief's high-powered sedan, drove to the scene of Tom's capture.

They found his sports car badly damaged. The right side was wedged against the utility pole, which was leaning at a crazy angle.

Ames whistled and shook his head. "Boy! You're lucky you got off with just a bruise, Tom!"

"You're telling me," the young inventor agreed ruefully.

After calling a repair garage to send out a wrecker, they drove to the Swifts' home. Mrs. Swift and Sandy, previously unaware of Tom's plight, were horrified to hear what had happened. The sight of Tom's bruise also upset them.

Tom did his best to allay their concern, but finally allowed himself to be hustled up to bed. Dr. Emerson, the Swifts' family physician, was immediately summoned to the house. He pronounced the bruise not serious, but advised that Tom remain quiet, at least for the rest of the day.

Bud came to visit the young inventor that evening, just as

Sandy was bringing up a tray. On it was a sizzling T-bone steak.

"Wow! Wish I could have that kind of service," Bud said jokingly. Then he became serious. "I'd sure like to meet that creep who snagged you, Tom. What a fiendish trick! You realize you might have been killed?"

"I realize it, all right," Tom said wryly.

The next morning Tom felt no ill effects from his grim adventure and insisted upon driving to Enterprises. He phoned Admiral Walter, whose report was bleak - the searchers had still gleaned no trace of the buried missile.

Refusing to be discouraged by the news, or lack of news, Tom went to his private laboratory and applied himself once again to the problem of building an "invisible" submarine. But again success eluded him.

At last Tom shook his head in disgust. "May as well get that haircut I started out for yesterday," he decided.

Before leaving, Tom phoned Phyl Newton to thank her for the gift of fruit and nuts she had brought over the previous evening after learning of his dangerous experience. They chatted for a while and wound up by making a date for lunch.

Tom drove back to town in the family car and got a haircut. Then he picked up Phyl at her home and took her to the yacht club. Here they lunched on the terrace overlooking the sparkling blue waters of Lake Carlopa.

The young inventor's spirits were high when he finally returned to his laboratory and buckled down to work.

"I'll lick this problem yet," he muttered. "Those enemies of ours are clever, but if they can produce an undetectable sub, there's no reason why I can't do the same."

Deep in thought, Tom idly fingered a microphone on his workbench.

"In fact," the young inventor mused, "why not go them one better? I'll invent a submarine that's not only invisible to sonar, but equipped to *see them*!"

CHAPTER XI

SQUARE-DANCE HOAX

Random hunches and circuit diagrams flashed through Tom's brain. "The job will boil down to blotting out sonar waves and piercing the enemy's own 'wave-trap defense,'" the young scientist concluded.

As Tom struggled with the problem, he lost all track of time. A door swung open and high-heeled boots clumped on the floor tiles. Tom looked up and saw the portly, aproned figure of Chow Winkler entering.

"Hi, boss! Can I borrow a radio?" Chow asked. "Kinda like a lil music while I wrassle them pots an' pans in the galley."

"Sure, pardner." Tom pointed toward a portable radio on a shelf nearby.

Chow's leathery face broke into a grin as he picked it up. "One o' them slick lil transistor doodads, eh?"

The cook flicked on the dial knob and the twangy strains of Hawaiian guitar music came throbbing out. A split second later the volume swelled as the same music echoed back to them from the two-room apartment adjoining the lab, where Tom ate and slept when engaged in some round-the-clock experiment.

Victor Appleton

Chow was startled by the blare. "You got a stereo hookup here, boss?" he inquired.

"Not exactly." Tom explained that the music had merely been picked up by the mike on his workbench, then fed into the adjoining apartment and amplified over a speaker there.

Chow grinned, snapping his fingers to the catchy melody. "Comes out even louder'n it does from the radio!"

"Yes, but the sound quality's not so good," Tom said. "You'd notice the difference with real stereo."

Chow walked out with the portable, crooning contentedly to the music.

Tom frowned, trying to get his train of thought to focus once more on the submarine problem. But for some reason the business with the microphone and the speaker in the next room kept lingering in his mind.

Suddenly Tom exclaimed aloud, "Say! I wonder if that's how the enemy sub blinds our sonar?"

The idea certainly seemed feasible. Suppose the submarine used a great many "microphones" - or receiving transducers - to pick up the sonar pulses beamed out by another craft trying to detect it? These impulses could then be passed on and sent out by speakers on the opposite side of the sub, and relayed along on their underwater path of travel.

Thus the sonar waves would appear to be striking no obstacle - and no echo would return to the sonarscopes on the search craft!

"Jumping jets!" Tom thumped his fist on the workbench in his excitement. "I'll bet that's the answer, all right!" He grinned. "Brand my boot heels, it's partly due to good old Chow!"

He grabbed a pencil and began sketching his idea on paper. It would be necessary to spot the receivers and transmitters all over the hull of the submarine. Diagrams and pages of scribbled computations followed the rough sketches.

An invisible sub - one that sonar pulses would seem to pass right through, as if nothing were there! "Seems so simple now that I have the key!" Tom said to himself elatedly.

Hours ticked by while he analyzed the wave action mathematically, then worked out a typical hookup for one of his jetmarines in a set of precise schematic drawings.

Finally the young inventor dropped his pencil, picked up the telephone, and dialed Bud Barclay.

"Hop over here, fly boy," Tom told his chum. "Something hot on the griddle!"

Bud arrived in a few moments. Tom showed him the drawings and explained his plan for dodging underwater detection. He also related how Chow's remarks about the radio music had sparked the idea.

His chum slapped him on the back. "Good going, Tom!"

"Let's fly right over to Fearing and see how it works on a jetmarine!" Tom proposed enthusiastically.

Bud grinned but made no move. He stood looking at Tom, arms folded and feet wide apart.

"Well, let's go, pal!" Tom urged impatiently, puzzled by Bud's lack of response.

"What about the square dance?"

Tom stopped short, feeling like a punctured balloon. He stared in dismay at his smiling, dark-haired copilot. "Good night! I forgot again!"

With a sigh, Tom added, "You're right, of course. We sure can't let the girls down twice. But at least let's get together all the gear we'll need when we *do* go to Fearing."

"I guess we'll have time for *that*," Bud conceded with a sympathetic grin.

Tom assembled a mass of electronic equipment and phoned various Enterprises' departments for other items. Bud helped to collect them, and the boys trucked the paraphernalia out to a hangar to be loaded aboard a Whirling Duck. Then they scootered back to the lab for a quick shower and change.

Twenty minutes later, in sport jackets, checked shirts, and slacks, the two chums hopped into Bud's red convertible. They picked up Sandy and Phyl and drove a little way into the country for dinner at a huge old farmhouse restaurant.

"Well, the evening's off to a good start," Sandy said with a happy laugh as they headed back along the lakeshore road to the yacht club.

"Hope I didn't put away too much fried chicken to sashay properly at the square dance," Bud remarked.

Tom chuckled. "Don't worry, pal. You always untangle those feet of yours when the fiddle strikes up!"

The blazing lights of the yacht club were reflected in the blue-black mirror of the boat basin. Bud parked and they went inside.

"Welcome, buckaroos!" Chow Winkler greeted them with an enthusiastic bellow as they entered the dance room.

The old cowpoke was splendidly dressed in a maroon satin shirt and white whipcord breeches tucked into shiny new boots. But instead of his usual sombrero, a chef's cap was perched on his head.

"Chow! You look marvelous!" Sandy said.

The cook blushed with pleasure. "You gals look purty enough to charm a hoot owl right off'n his perch!" he shot back. Both Phyl and Sandy were wearing gay calico dresses that had full swirling skirts.

The room was decked out with colored bunting and twisted crepe-paper streamers. And at one end of the dance room, Chow had rigged up a model of a Western chuck wagon.

"Real atmosphere!" Tom said admiringly. "Chow, you've done us proud!"

"Thanks, boss." The cook, who had asked especially to take charge of the decorations, glowed at the praise. Then he became serious. "But what's keepin' that dad-blamed fiddler?"

The guests soon began to stream in, but half an hour went by, and Lester Morris and his fellow musicians had not arrived.

"I'd better phone his house," Tom decided worriedly.

Mrs. Morris answered. She seemed surprised at Tom's call. "Why, my husband's playing at a party over in Carterton this evening," she said. "Are you sure you engaged him for tonight?"

"I'm positive," Tom replied.

"Just a moment, please. I'll look in his date book to see if there's been a mistake."

A minute later her voice came over the line again. "I'm terribly sorry, Mr. Swift, but your name isn't listed anywhere on Lester's schedule."

The others saw from Tom's face as he hung up that something was wrong.

"What gives?" Bud asked anxiously.

"No music for one thing." Tom reported what Mrs. Morris had told him.

"But you hired the guy!" Bud protested. "And Sandy and I talked to his agent!"

Tom was already piecing together the mystery. He shook his head thoughtfully. "I'm sure now the whole deal was a hoax, Bud," he declared. "Both the first call that supposedly came from Lester Morris, and the second one asking me to come here and talk things over."

By not responding to the second call in person, Tom went on, he had probably saved himself from being waylaid or kidnaped by his enemies.

"Thank goodness!" Sandy exclaimed. "Still, that creepy Len Unger was trying to get information from us."

"But how did your enemy know about the dance, Tom?" Phyl Newton put in.

Sandy snapped her fingers. "I know! I'll bet it was when we went shopping for our dresses, Phyl, right after the boys invited us! The department store was full of people - almost anyone might have heard us discussing the dance!"

"Especially if he was already trailing you to pick up bits of useful information," Tom agreed.

Bud whipped out a handkerchief and mopped his face nervously. "The question is what do we do now, chums? A roomful of guests and no music!"

"Relax, pardners!" Chow broke in cheerfully. "Just keep things goin' for a spell, an' I'll fix things up pronto!"

Doffing his chef's cap, Chow hustled out to his parked jeep and took off with a roar. Mystified but hopeful, Tom, Bud, and Phyl did their best to entertain the guests. Sandy had rushed to the telephone. In twenty minutes Chow came rushing back.

"Hey! He has a fiddle!" Bud exclaimed.

Mounting the platform, the stout cowpoke raised his hands and shouted for attention.

"Ladies an' gents, we'll start off with that good old dance known as the Texas Star!"

As everyone took his place, Chow tuned up hastily. Then he tucked the fiddle under his chin, stomped out the rhythm, and launched into a lively rendition of "Turkey in the Straw" while he called out the accompaniment:

> *"Gals to the middle, then back so far!*
> *Gents step up for a clockwise star!*
> *Now shift hands and twirl t'other way,*
> *We'll keep on dancin' till the break o' day...."*

The dance number finally ended to thunderous applause. Chow, puffing and red-faced but wreathed in smiles, was soon ready for another. Half an hour later, a dance band of high school boys, hastily summoned by Sandy, arrived to spell the Texan.

The irrepressible chef, however, continued to call out most of the numbers and proved to be the hero of the evening. He gained even more acclaim for his delicious French fried potatoes and "steerburgers" served during the pause for refreshments.

"Oh, Chow! What would we ever do without you?" Sandy said, and the cook beamed.

Suddenly, in the midst of the lively chatter and laughter, the dance floor was plunged into total darkness!

Phyl clung fearfully to her escort. "Tom!" she gasped. "This is another trick of your enemy's to harm you!"

CHAPTER XII

DETECTION TEST

"Don't worry, Phyl. It may be only a blown fuse," Tom tried to assure the fearful girl.

But Tom was worried himself. Not only might he be in danger, but it could involve his friends!

Nevertheless, he raised his voice above the excited babble. "Please be calm, everyone! We'll have the lights on again in a jiffy!"

Taking Phyl by the hand, Tom groped his way toward the main door.

"Let's check the switch," he murmured, and ran his hand over the wall near the door. He located the metal plate and flipped the switch.

The lights went on! Good-natured cheers arose. Bud, grinning but puzzled, left Sandy's side long enough to come over and speak to Tom.

"What happened?"

"I guess some practical joker clicked off the switch."

Bud suddenly caught sight of a stout youth in a plaid shirt and blue jeans, who was standing in a nearby corner. He was shaking all over with half-stifled merriment.

"There's the wise guy! Rock Harriman!"

Rock, an all-star tackle on the Shopton High football team, was well known for his pranks and practical jokes. Bud rushed over.

"Okay! Confess!" the husky young flier roared in a jokingly ferocious tone.

"Don't get sore!" Rock gasped between chuckles. "I couldn't resist. Boy, did you hear everyone squeal when the lights went out?"

Tom grinned in relief. "How about another dance, Phyl?"

As the music struck up again, he squeezed Phyl's hand. "I sure appreciate your concern, even if I didn't rate it."

Phyl blushed as she returned the squeeze. "You rate with me," she confided shyly.

The festivities finally ended after a thoroughly enjoyable evening. Both Sandy and Phyl declared to their dates that it more than made up for the forgotten beach party.

"But let's not wait too long for the next date," Sandy warned playfully.

"Okay, that's a deal," Bud promised.

The next morning at the plant Tom called on Harlan Ames. He told of the sinister hoax by the caller who had passed himself off as Lester Morris. The security chief promised to investigate.

"I'll tip off the police about Len Unger," Ames added. "If they can find him, we may be able to crack this case wide open."

Tom telephoned Bud, Hank Sterling, and Arv Hanson to meet him at the helijet hangar. The four took off in one of the Swifts' Whirling Ducks, which was standing by loaded and ready. Soon they landed on Fearing Island, where Tom would try out his antidetection invention.

"What'll we use for a test sub, skipper?" Hank asked as they drove toward the docks.

"A jetmarine," Tom replied.

A truck with engineers and technicians was following the jeep. It carried the equipment which Tom and Bud had assembled the previous day.

When they arrived at the docks, Tom gathered the men in a loading shed. He showed them his drawings and explained how his "sonar-blinding" setup would operate.

"Don't let the diagrams fool you. The basic idea is very simple. We absorb all sonar impulses that hit the ship and transmit them out the opposite side of the hull, instead of letting a ping bounce back and show up on the sonarscope of any hostile sub on the lookout for us."

Most of the job, he went on, would be tedious detail work. It would consist of attaching hundreds of mikes and speakers all over the hull to pick up and transmit the sonar pulses. The mikes would be receiving transducers and the speakers would be transmitting transducers.

"The leads from them," Tom ended, "will be centralized in a single electronic control unit inside the ship. I'll handle that part of it."

"Great idea, Tom!" Arv Hanson said admiringly.

"But what a job it'll be rigging those transducers," put in one of the technicians.

Tom nodded wryly. "You're right, Danny. If this experiment works out, though, I think I can lick that problem on future installations."

The young inventor explained that he hoped to find a way to mold the transducers into a continuous plastic sheet. This could be applied to the hull of a submarine in a single operation.

"But this time we'll have to do it the hard way," Tom added with an apologetic grin.

A jetmarine was hoisted into drydock and the work crew swarmed over it, rigging the transducers. Would his experiment succeed? Tom wondered. Hopefully, he set to work assembling the electronic control unit.

Bud helped the men on the hull for a while, then descended through the hatch to see how Tom was progressing.

"I'd go gaga trying to keep track of those circuits," Bud said, as he watched Tom installing the delicate transistors and other components with an electric soldering gun.

The young inventor grinned. "It'll be simple enough when the control unit's all put together," he replied. "Just a single on-off switch and one test circuit."

By noon, after working at a frenzied pace, the job was done. Tom thanked each one of the men personally. Then everyone went to eat lunch.

After the meal, Hank Sterling asked, "How about a detection test to see how she works?"

"Coming right up," Tom said. " Want to skipper the

jetmarine, Bud?"

"Sure do!"

"Okay. Pick out a couple of men for a crew and take her down." Tom produced a hydrographic chart of the waters around Fearing and marked out a test area. "Cruise around there for an hour and we'll try to spot you in the *Sea Hound*."

"Hide and seek, eh?" Bud grinned and snapped a salute, then left to supervise the relaunching of the jetmarine.

For his crew, Bud chose Mel Flagler and another man. Mel was an experienced jetmariner who had gone on the Swift expedition to Aurum City, the underwater ruins of a lost civilization. Here Tom had used his spectromarine selector to restore the ancient buildings.

Tom, Hank, and Arv went back to the airfield and soon took off in the diving seacopter. Landing on the water, they submerged and began the undersea detection test.

Tom manned the sonarscope personally, eager to conduct as careful a search as possible.

"Getting any blips, skipper?" Hank called out from his post at the *Sea Hound*'s controls.

"Not a ping, Hank. The system seems to be working out even better than I'd hoped."

Tom felt a glow of satisfaction. He explained, however, that the jetmarine's transparent nose pane - which had to be left unprotected for the pilot's visibility - offered one vulnerable spot to sonar detection.

"But a little smart maneuvering can cover up that angle," Tom added. "Try the hydrophones, Arv, and see if you can hear 'em."

Victor Appleton

The chief modelmaker slipped on the earphones and listened intently. For another ten or fifteen minutes they probed about with no sound trace of the "invisible" jetmarine.

But presently Arv snapped his fingers to catch Tom's attention. "Got her, skipper!"

Tom took over the hydrophones. Sure enough, his ears could make out the faint hum of the jetmarine's atomic turbines. Tom directed Hank toward the sound, then ordered him to switch on the *Sea Hound*'s powerful search beam.

The light cut a path of radiance through the murky dark-green waters. Dead ahead, the jetmarine could be seen gliding across their field of view.

"Your system blinded our sonar okay, skipper," Hank commented, "but this proves she could still be spotted by enemy listening devices."

Tom refused to be discouraged. He ordered Hank to return to base and wait for Bud. Meanwhile, the young inventor applied himself to the problem of how to mask the sub's noise.

"How about it, pal?" Bud asked, when he reported aboard the seacopter a while later.

Tom explained the results of the test and the need for an added safeguard against hydrophone detection. "Think I see a simple way out, though," he added with a pleased chuckle.

"Natch! With a brain like yours, it's a cinch," Bud quipped. "Explain, professor."

"Well, we can never do away with the noise of a sub's propulsion machinery," Tom began. "That goes without saying. So we'll have to camouflage it - lose it in the underwater jungle noises, so to speak."

Bud scratched his head. "How do we do that?"

"By amplifying the natural undersea sounds all about it," Tom explained. "Fish and all forms of underwater life make a background noise over the hydrophones, you know."

As Bud nodded, Tom went on, "So we simply step up the volume till the sub's own noise gets drowned out or 'wasted' in all the racket."

This could be done, he concluded, with fairly simple amplifying equipment. Bud, Hank, and Arv were jubilant at the idea.

"Nice going," Bud said. "How soon can we give it a try?"

"Soon as I can rig up the amplifier," Tom promised.

In less than two hours they were ready to submerge again. Zimby Cox joined the crew. Bud suggested taking along hydrolungs in case of any need for tinkering with the transducers or amplifying equipment.

This time, the jetmarine scored perfectly on the test, successfully eluding all the *Sea Hound*'s efforts to detect it. Tom returned happily to base, feeling that the antidetection problem was now solved. The jetmarine, however, failed to appear.

"That's funny. The test was over at four-fifteen," Tom murmured.

"Maybe Bud surfaced out at sea somewhere," Arv Hanson suggested.

Repeated radio calls brought no response. Tom, now seriously worried, took the seacopter down again for another search, hoping that Bud would have switched off the antidetection gear by this time. But neither sonarscope nor listening devices revealed the slightest clue.

Tom, Hank, and Arv exchanged fearful glances. Had the jetmarine foundered on the ocean bottom - perhaps fouled somehow by Tom's new invention? Or had Bud and his crew fallen victim to the enemy?

CHAPTER XIII

ENEMY FROGMEN

At the end of the test period, Bud had prepared to bring the jetmarine to the surface. But just as he was about to blow the ballast tanks, Mel Flagler sang out a warning from the sonarscope.

"Whoa! Hold it, skipper! I think we have company on the starboard beam!"

Bud jerked his head around in surprise. "You mean the *Sea Hound*?"

"No, she surfaced," Mel reported. "Can't make this out yet, but it could be another sub."

Bud turned the controls over to Zimby Cox. Then he rushed to the scope and examined the blip. "Seems to be moving away from us on a westerly course. It's about two miles from here."

He donned the hydrophone earset and listened. "It's no seacopter, nor a jetmarine either," he announced presently.

"A Navy sub, maybe?" suggested Zimby.

Bud shrugged. "Let's find out." He ordered a change of course, hard to the right, and gunned the jets to bring the jetmarine directly on the mystery object's trail.

Victor Appleton

"It's a sub, all right," he said a short time later, listening again over the hydrophones.

"Pretty close to Fearing Island, isn't it?" put in Mel Flagler. "That's a government-restricted area."

Bud nodded grimly. "But staying just out of sonar range from the base."

The jetmarine closed steadily on its quarry. In a few minutes they were able to make it out dimly through the cabin window, dead ahead.

"That's sure no U.S. Navy sub that I know of," Bud said. "Probably an enemy snooper."

"What if they spot us?" Zimby asked.

Bud chuckled. "That's the beauty of it, pal! Don't forget. With this new antidetection gear we're invisible to them. At least as long as they don't run into us or we into them," he added.

"Or unless they have superdetection equipment we don't know about," cautioned Mel Flagler.

As they talked, the unidentified submarine was bearing steadily toward the mainland. Fathometer soundings showed it was on a steep upward slope of the continental shelf.

Presently a foaming gush of bubbles showed that the sub ahead was blowing its tanks. The jetmarine followed as it surfaced and Bud hastily manned the periscope.

"What're they up to?" Mel asked tensely.

"Don't know yet, but the hatch is opening," Bud reported. Suddenly he gave an excited gasp. "Jumpin' jets! They're sending out a couple of frogmen!"

Bud's companions were electrified by the news.

"Spies!" Zimby exclaimed.

"What do we do now?" piped up Mack Avery, the third man in Bud's crew. "Hadn't we better radio the Coast Guard and the FBI?"

Bud wrenched away from the eyepiece. "I have another idea! Any of you fellows game to go with me and capture those spies?"

All three of his companions volunteered eagerly. Bud chose Mel Flagler, then took another sight through the periscope.

"The sub's submerging again," he reported. "That'll give us a clear field. Zimby, you and Mack keep an eye on that baby while we're gone, and be plenty careful she doesn't spot you!"

"Roger! And take this roll of wire to tie up your prisoners."

Hastily Bud and Mel changed into swimming trunks and donned hydrolungs. They went out through the air lock, plunged into the bracing salt water, and switched on their ion-drive units.

"Can you see 'em?" Mel asked over his mike.

"Not yet. Let's speed up before we lose 'em completely!"

Both pushed their ion drives to capacity, scanning the water ahead in all directions.

"There they are!" Bud exclaimed presently. He pointed to two tiny figures, barely visible in the distance.

"Wow! They're sure not wasting any time!" Mel muttered. "Let's step on it, Bud! They'll be ashore in a minute!"

Victor Appleton

A darting school of sea bass screened the figures briefly from view. As the fish flickered past, Mel and Bud saw the frogmen breast-stroke up toward the surface and break water.

Bud and Mel followed. Ahead lay a barren stretch of beach, humped with sand dunes. It was skirted beyond by a thick fringe of trees.

"They certainly picked a perfect spot for a sneak landing!" Bud thought. The beach seemed totally deserted, with no sign of human habitation.

By this time, the frogmen were scrambling ashore. Within moments, Bud and Mel were on their heels. The raiders whirled in dismay as they caught the sound of footsteps rushing up behind them through the sand.

Bud and Mel hurled themselves forward, each dropping a man with a flying tackle. All four went down in a struggling, kicking tangle of arms and legs.

The battle was rough but short. Bud and Mel had the advantage of surprise, and soon pommeled and grappled their foes into submission.

Bud, astride his opponent's chest with knees pinning the man's arms, unlooped from his belt the wire he had brought.

"Here! Take some of this and wire your man's wrists together!" Bud told Mel.

When the frogmen were safely bound, Bud and Mel allowed them to stand up. Neither captive tried to escape.

"Now, my sneaky friends, talk!" Bud snapped. "What kind of a sightseeing trip did you plan?"

The frogmen's jaws remained tightly clamped. Both looked flushed and sullen as they faced their captors.

"Got their lips zipped, I guess," Mel said disgustedly.

Bud decided to try another tack. "Doesn't matter," he said carelessly. "We know they're pals of the Mirovs."

Both men started as if they had been stung. Bud followed up quickly, hoping to prod them into some unguarded remark.

"Just as we thought!" he snarled. "A couple of low-down Brungarian rebels! And up to their usual amateurish spy stunts!"

The raiders' eyes blazed, but they maintained silence. Both, however, kept darting looks of keen interest at the Americans' hydrolung gear.

Just as Bud was wondering how he could get the prisoners to the nearest police headquarters, a jeep came bouncing into view across the sand.

"Hey! Police!" Mel exclaimed with a happy grin.

"We're in luck," Bud said. "They can take these creeps off our hands."

The jeep braked to a halt a few yards away, and two uniformed officers hopped out.

"What's going on here?" said one, who was wearing a sergeant's stripes. The jeep had the words BEACH PATROL stenciled on it in white paint.

"We just nailed these two Brungarian frogmen," Bud explained. "A sub put them ashore - probably as spies or saboteurs. They won't talk to us, but maybe you can pump them at headquarters."

The startled sergeant turned a cold eye on the two prisoners. "Got anything to say for yourselves?" When neither answered, he unholstered his revolver and covered them. "Better take off those wires and put bracelets on them, Mike," he told his fellow officer.

The frogmen were handcuffed with cool efficiency and bundled into the jeep. Meanwhile, the sergeant turned back to Bud and Mel.

"You fellows come along too," he ordered.

"But we haven't got time," Bud protested. "Our own sub's waiting right offshore and we want to tail the sub that brought those guys here! We're from the Swift rocket base."

"Any identification?" the sergeant asked.

"How *could* we have in this getup?" Mel retorted.

"That's what I thought. So get moving," the sergeant barked.

Reluctantly, Bud and Mel hopped onto the running board and clung to the bouncing jeep as it sped to the nearby town of Sandbank. At headquarters they were questioned by the local police chief.

"If you'll call Swift Enterprises at Shopton, sir, Mr. Swift - or Harlan Ames of the plant security department - will vouch for us," Bud said.

The chief picked up the telephone and soon had Mr. Swift on the line. After speaking to him briefly, he passed the phone to Bud so the scientist could identify his voice.

"That's Bud Barclay, all right. He's one of our most trusted employees," Mr. Swift told the chief after hearing Bud's story.

The officer promised to release Mel and Bud at once. Before doing so, however, he took them into the adjoining office where the two frogmen were being questioned.

"Any luck?" the chief asked the sergeant.

Sergeant Gryce shook his head in disgust. "Not much. They did admit they came in a sub, but they claim it didn't wait to pick them up."

The police chief shot a few questions of his own at the men, but they answered either in curt monosyllables or not at all.

"Look, sir," Bud put in, "if they're telling the truth about their sub not waiting, our jetmarine may have chased it. That means Mel and I are stranded here. Could you have your men wait for us on the beach till we find out?"

"Gladly," the chief replied. "You two have done a fine day's work."

After the prisoners had been locked up to be handed over to the FBI, the two Beach Patrol officers drove Bud and Mel back to the area where they had landed. Just as the jeep turned down the dirt road leading to the shore, Bud's keen eyes spotted a lurking figure in the distance.

"Stop, please!" Bud said, tapping the driver on the shoulder.

As the jeep halted, Bud pointed toward the beach. A man was crouching behind a sand dune, with a large fish basket beside him. The sergeant, puzzled, took out a pair of binoculars to study the situation. Fortunately, the jeep was still screened by trees, and the crouching man evidently did not realize he had been seen.

"What's in the basket?" Bud asked. "Could it be clothes?"

"Sure looks like it," the sergeant said, passing over the binoculars.

After a brief look, Bud explained the hunch that had occurred to him. "I'll bet that guy's waiting with clothes for the frogmen. He probably got here late and doesn't realize they've been nabbed!"

"Well, he'll soon find out," the police driver said grimly. He was about to start up the jeep when Bud stopped him again.

"Wait! You have no proof that's what he's here for," Bud pointed out.

The pilot suggested that the police keep out of sight while he and Mel approached the man in their swimming gear. "If that stranger takes the bait, we'll really have the goods on him!" Bud concluded.

"Smart idea, son," the sergeant said with a dry chuckle. "Go to it!"

Bud and Mel circled widely through the trees, took a quick dip in the water, then approached along the beach as if they had just landed and were searching for someone.

To their delight, the man rose from behind the sand dune and hailed them. Bud and Mel hurried over to him.

"You have clothes for us?" Bud asked. "We just came ashore from the sub!"

"Yeah, right here," the man said in English with no trace of an accent. "Thought I'd missed you."

"Thanks, pal - that's all we want to know!"

The man gaped in comic dismay as Bud pounced on him and pinned him to the ground. Moments later, the two police officers rushed up and handcuffed him.

"Hey! What's the big idea?" the man stammered. "I ain't done nothing. Just got a phone call this morning, offering me fifty bucks to bring two sets of clothes down to the beach at five o'clock for a couple of divers."

"Tell that to the FBI!" snapped the sergeant.

When the officers had departed with their new prisoner, Bud and Mel, both grinning, dived into the surf and headed out to sea.

In a few minutes they were sure they were at the right spot to meet the jetmarine. But it was gone!

CHAPTER XIV

A PROPAGANDA BLITZ

As the *Sea Hound* returned to Fearing Island from its search for Bud's jetmarine, Tom was beside himself with worry. Had his experiment cost the lives of his best friend and the other crewmen aboard?

"I'll never forgive myself if anything's happened to them!" Tom muttered bleakly.

Hank Sterling squeezed the young inventor's arm. "You know Bud's high spirits, skipper," he said. "He may have taken off on some crazy lark."

"Sure! A whale hunt, maybe!" Arv Hanson wisecracked, trying to lighten the gloom.

Tom forced a grin, but he remained heavy-hearted as they neared the base. His only hope now was that a radio message from the jetmarine might have been picked up while they were gone.

As soon as the seacopter was moored, Tom leaped ashore. The crewmen on the docks had no news to report, so Tom piled into a jeep with Arv and sped off to the Fearing communications center. Hank remained aboard the *Sea Hound* to secure all gear.

Churning along the graveled road, Tom and Arv passed the launching area. Huge, needle-nosed cargo rockets and the mighty spaceship *Titan* loomed against the sky. Tom's moon-voyaging *Challenger* and his more recent space craft the *Cosmic Sailer* were also based there.

"Going to alert the Navy for a search?" Arv inquired as they reached the communications building.

Tom nodded and braked the jeep to a screeching halt. "Coast Guard too. They can pass the word to commercial shipping to be on the lookout."

A telephone rang as he hurried into the office.

"For you," the clerk said, looking up at Tom. "Nice timing!"

Tom grabbed the phone. His face widened into a grin. "Bud! You seagoing jet stream! What happened?"

Arv grinned, too, in relief.

"Your antidetection gear worked so well we vanished right out of the ocean!" Bud replied with a chuckle. Turning serious, he reported how his jetmarine had trailed the mysterious intruder and how he and Mel had captured the two Brungarian frogmen and their shore contact.

"Nice going, pal!" Tom exclaimed.

"But here's the catch," Bud went on. "When we took off again in our hydrolungs to go back aboard ship, the jetmarine was gone!"

"Maybe she's trailing the enemy sub," Tom conjectured.

"That's what I'm hoping," Bud said uneasily. "Trouble is, our subs aren't armed, and who knows about that Brungarian job? The way they sling missiles around, anything could happen if she spots the jetmarine."

Tom frowned. "I'll organize a search right away. Where are you calling from?"

"Police headquarters at Sandbank."

"Okay. Take it easy, and I'll send a whirlybird to pick you up," Tom promised.

"And don't forget some clothes," Bud added with a chuckle. "Mel and I are getting chilly."

"Right!" Tom hung up and gave Arv Hanson a quick briefing.

Then he phoned the base airfield to dispatch a helicopter. He also contacted the nearest Coast Guard station and put through a long-distance call to Navy Headquarters in Washington to request help in searching for the jetmarine. Finally he and Arv headed back to the submarine docks in the jeep.

A flurry of activity followed as Tom detailed ships for the search and rounded up crews. He was interrupted by a phone call in the loading shed. It was the control-tower operator.

"One of our drone planes has spotted a sub approaching, skipper," the operator reported.

"What bearing?" Tom demanded excitedly.

"One-seven-six." Tom was about to hang up and grab a pair of binoculars when the operator added hastily, "Wait! It's responding to our radio challenge!... That's ours, all right!"

Tom dashed out of the shed and scanned the sea to the southward. Sure enough, a jetmarine had surfaced and was speeding toward the sub docks. Minutes later, Tom was shaking hands warmly with Zimby Cox and Mack Avery.

"Is Bud okay?" was Zimby's first question.

"Right! I just heard from him," Tom replied. "He and Mel captured those enemy frogmen and a copter's on the way to pick them up. What happened
to you fellows?"

Zimby confirmed Bud's guess that they had taken off in pursuit of the enemy craft.

"We figured Bud and Mel could make out on their own," Zimby explained. "And we thought the sub's course or actions might tip us off to its nationality. Also, if it tried any sabotage or mine-planting, we could radio the Navy."

Instead, Cox went on, the mysterious craft had proceeded to a point about ten miles offshore where it rendezvoused with another submarine.

"And get this, skipper!" Mack Avery put in. "The other sub was undetectable! We were close enough to get a peek at it, but we couldn't ping it on the sonarscope."

"That figures," Tom said grimly. "Those frogmen were apparently Brungarians."

Zimby Cox related that a man had transferred from the undetectable submarine to the one they had been following. The first sub had then headed out to sea, as if to cross the ocean back to its home base. The other had departed on a course toward the South Atlantic.

"Probably back to the lost missile area. At least that's the way we figured it," Zimby added.

"And neither sub spotted you?" Tom questioned.

Zimby grinned wryly. "We might not be here if they *had* detected us. But I'm pretty sure they didn't. Anyhow, they

Victor Appleton

gave no sign."

Tom was doubly elated at the news. His antidetection gear had evidently worked perfectly in a showdown test with the enemy, even at close range. Moreover, if the second sub was returning to the South Atlantic, it seemed likely that the enemy, too, had not yet located the precious missile with its data from Jupiter.

"You guys rate Navy medals," Tom told Zimby and Mack jubilantly. "Come on back to Shopton with me and I'll buy you the juiciest steaks in town!"

Before leaving the base, Tom called the Coast Guard and the Navy to cancel his search request. He also telephoned a full report on the enemy submarines to Admiral Walter.

After hanging up, Tom decided on another move. "Our antidetection gear seems to have panned out pretty well," he told Hank. "I think we should make use of it right away. By sending that jetmarine to the South Atlantic, we might get a line on enemy activities down there."

Hank was in favor of the idea. He volunteered to prepare the jetmarine for a cruise and take off from Fearing that very night.

"Thanks," Tom said with a parting handshake. "Keep us posted if you learn anything."

Meanwhile, Bud and Mel Flagler had arrived at the base by helicopter. They and their two shipmates flew back to the mainland with Tom and Arv for a celebration dinner in town.

The next morning found the young inventor hard at work in his private laboratory. He was tapping his head with his slide rule and frowning at a blackboard scrawled with equations when Bud dropped in for a visit.

"What now, inventor boy?" his copilot asked. "Don't you ever give that brain of yours a rest?"

"Oh, hi, Bud!" Tom looked around absent-mindedly. "I'm just trying to figure out a way to crack the Brungarians' antisonar system."

"Good night!" Bud sank down on a lab stool. "You've come up with a way to make our own subs undetectable. Isn't that enough?"

Tom shook his head. "Not if we want to keep track of those sneaks. And I think I see a way to do it."

"How?"

"So far, I have been thinking about refining our own search sonar." Tom explained that the new system he had in mind would send out a *complex* pulse - that is, an underwater sound wave with many harmonics instead of a single tone, sharp-peaked sound impulse.

"This will make it less likely that their antidetection gear will absorb all of it," Tom went on. "What's not absorbed will return as an echo. I'm also going to modify our receivers. But I've still not worked that out."

Bud nodded, his forehead puckered in a look of concentration. "So - ?"

"So our sonar picks up all that hash, and by means of a computer setup filters out the sub's real echo from the shadow reflections."

"Hey! Sounds pretty cute," Bud said.

Tom broke into a dry chuckle. "Right - *if* I can do it." After that job, Tom added, he hoped to adapt his own antidetection methods to make hydrolung wearers safe from underwater detection. "And if the Jupiter prober hasn't been found by that time, Bud, I'm going to request the Navy to let us take over the search alone."

Bud gave a whistle of excitement at the possibility of new undersea adventures ahead. "Count me in, pal!"

The two boys broke off their conversation a short time later and went back to the Administration Building for lunch with Tom's father.

Mr. Swift greeted them with a smile as they entered the big double office. "Glad you could join me, boys! Chow's laid out quite a feast for us today."

Three places had been set at the conference table, and an appetizing repast of sizzling ham and sweet potatoes waited in covered dishes on a lunch cart nearby.

"Mmm!" Bud inhaled the aroma. "Good chow from good old Chow!"

Tom switched on the videophone screen to a private channel to catch the noon news while they ate. The newscaster wore a look of excitement as he spoke without pausing for the usual commercial.

"The Brungarian government has just scored a propaganda bombshell!" he reported. "In a news announcement released less than half an hour ago, they stated that their Navy has perfected an *undetectable submarine!*"

The Swifts and Bud froze, openmouthed, at the newscaster's words.

"No need to tell you what this could mean to American security," he went on. "If enemy subs slipped through our continental defenses, their missiles could devastate the United States with scarcely an instant's warning! The whole country's been rocked by the announcement. An official comment by our Defense Department is expected at any moment."

"Sufferin' satellites!" Bud gulped.

Mr. Swift nodded. "It's a great propaganda stroke. But I wonder why they've chosen to reveal their secret at this time."

Tom said thoughtfully, "Dad, do you suppose they've realized the fact that we *know* about their antisonar gear?"

"Could be, son. They may figure that since the secret is out already, they may as well play it up for all it's worth." The elder scientist paused and frowned. "Or it might be intended to force our hand."

"You mean in hopes of getting us to reveal whether or not we have an antidetection system ourselves?" As his father nodded, Tom scowled. "If so, that sub yesterday may have been observing our tests."

The telephone rang and Tom leaped to answer it. The caller was Dan Perkins of the *Shopton Evening Bulletin*.

"You can guess why I'm calling, Tom," the editor said. "How about a statement from you Swifts on this Brungarian sub story?"

"We found it very interesting," Tom said politely but noncommittally. Parrying further questions, he hung up as soon as possible.

Mr. Swift approved Tom's policy of silence. Almost immediately the phone began ringing again with a succession of calls from other newspapers and wire services. Tom dashed off a brief, general statement and instructed Miss Trent to give it to all further callers.

"Maybe this is a good time to make a private announcement to you fellows," Mr. Swift said to the two boys, his eyes twinkling. "Do you recall my telling you that Doc Simpson had isolated an unknown vitamin from the space plants? Well, we've now discovered that this vitamin can condition the human body to stay under water indefinitely. Doc is putting some up in capsule form."

Both Tom and Bud gave whoops of glee at this news.

"Dad, you've helped overcome one of the big problems in our search for the lost missile!" Tom exclaimed.

CHAPTER XV

MOUNTAIN HIKE

"After adequate doses of your space vitamin, Dad, a skin diver could tackle almost any undersea job in my hydrolung!" Tom exclaimed. "He wouldn't be subjected to any antiosmosis troubles with his body tissues."

His father nodded. "For the first time, man might become a *truly marine creature!*"

"Wow! Think of it!" Bud gasped excitedly. "With Tom's hydrolung and a knife to hunt his own food, he could practically live in the sea!"

"That's no farfetched dream, Bud." Tom's steel-blue eyes flashed at the thought of new fields of scientific conquest. "This discovery of Dad's and Doc Simpson's opens up some really amazing possibilities."

Most important at the moment, the vitamin would be a great boon in carrying out search and digging operations for the Jupiter prober. With fresh enthusiasm, Tom returned to his laboratory to work on the new sonar gear. In his own mind, he had already named it a "quality analyzer sonar," since that exactly described the way it would function.

"Hmm, let's see," Tom mused as he settled down at his workbench, pencil in hand. "Besides a regular sonarscope, I'll need at least three units for the gear."

First, he would need an oscillator to produce the complex pulse. Next, of course, an oscilloscope to check the pulse as it was beamed out. Last - but highly important - a correlation calculator.

This latter unit would compare the original pulse with the returning echoes. If an echo had a high enough "standard of acceptance" - that is, if its quality was very near the original pulse, it would show up on the screen in the normal way. If the echo came back blurred, or if "shadow echoes" showed up, these would be separated and appear on the screen colored red.

"Whew!" Tom sighed as he realized the complicated job of circuit design that lay ahead. "This sure is going to burn some midnight oil!"

The young inventor worked all afternoon at a furious pace, breaking off toward dinnertime to telephone his mother that he would be staying overnight at the lab. After a hasty meal, he resumed his layout job at the drawing board and by midnight had finished designing his quality analyzer sonar.

Whipping off his eyeshade, Tom went into the apartment next door and stretched out to snatch a few hours' sleep. But as usual when in the midst of an exciting new project, he was too keyed up to rest for long.

Before daylight, Tom was back at his workbench ready to begin assembling the units of his new sonar gear. Later he phoned Chow but scarcely paused to eat when the cook arrived with his order.

"Brand my solar stovepipe!" Chow scolded. "Take time to eat your vittles properly, boss!"

"Hmm?... Oh, sure." Tom looked up and grinned.

The stout old Texan stomped out, shaking his head.

As the morning wore on, the pace at which Tom had been working began to tell on the young inventor. His head nodded again and again. Gradually he fell forward into an exhausted doze.

The next thing Tom knew, he was sailing through the air, high above Swift Enterprises. Lake Carlopa was a tiny blue puddle below, and the town of Shopton a mere cluster of toy buildings in the distance.

"Good grief!" Tom exclaimed with a gulp. "What's keeping me up?"

He was floating freely, without the support of any aircraft - or even one of his amazing force-ray repelatrons!

The discovery triggered off disaster. Like a character in a movie cartoon, now that he knew he had nothing to support him, Tom instantly went plunging downward - down, down, straight into the lake!

Splash!

Tom gasped and shuddered and shook his head like a drenched terrier.

Another splash! As Tom brought his eyes into focus, he realized he was back at his workbench in the laboratory. Chow was standing in front of him, holding a half-empty pail of water, ready to splash him again!

"Hey! Cut it out!" Tom cried out, jerking bolt upright. Then, as he saw the disturbed look on Chow's face, Tom burst out laughing. "Okay. Relax, old-timer! Guess I was dreaming."

"Brand my snake oil!" Chow said. "You looked so pale an' pasty, you had me plumb scared, Tom! I couldn't wake you

Victor Appleton

nohow!" Worriedly the cook added, "What you need is a good beefsteak and some sunshine. You been under water too long."

"In more ways than one!" Tom chuckled as he grabbed a towel and dried himself off.

The beefsteak, with crisp golden-brown French fried potatoes, was already at hand on Chow's lunch cart. Tom ate with a hearty appetite and the stout chef went off, secretly plotting to arrange the second half of his prescription.

When he reached the galley, Chow plucked the wall phone off its hook and called Bud at an airfield hangar. After a brisk conversation, he hung up, grinning contentedly.

At one o'clock Bud came bursting into Tom's laboratory. "Snap to, skipper!" he announced. "You have company!"

Tom looked up from his work in surprise.

"*Ta-daaa!*" Bud sang out, imitating a trumpet flourish.

Sandy and Phyl Newton marched in, smiling.

"Boy, this *is* a surprise!" Tom got up to greet them. "A mighty pleasant one. But what's the occasion?"

"The occasion is that you're coming on a mountain hike with us, out in the nice fresh air and sunshine!" Sandy informed him.

"And please don't argue," Phyl said with a giggle. "It's for your own good - not to mention ours."

"I suppose Chow Winkler put you up to this." Tom grinned.

"Never mind that," Sandy said sternly. "Just come along quietly. It's a beautiful day."

Tom glanced at his workbench cluttered with drawings and electronic gear. "Well, okay, since you're twisting my arm," he agreed. "I guess it might clear my brain at that."

"Now you're talking." Bud clapped Tom on the back and propelled him toward the two girls, who promptly seized his arms before he might change his mind.

On their way to the door, however, the telephone rang. Tom insisted upon answering it, in spite of the girls' scolding.

"Tom Swift Jr. talking."

"This is Chief Slater, Tom," said the voice at the other end of the line. "Dimitri Mirov wants to see you. I don't know what's up, but he might be ready to tell something worth while. Could you drop by?"

"Sure thing, Chief. Right away!" Tom hung up, excited by the thought that the Brungarian might be about to reveal an important secret. "Mind stopping by police headquarters first?" he asked his friends.

Minutes later, Bud's red convertible pulled up in front of the gray stone building. Tom jumped out and dashed up the granite steps.

"I've had Mirov transferred to a cell by himself," Chief Slater said as he took Tom back to see him. "Figured he might talk more freely away from his pals."

The prisoner, however, showed no eagerness to do so at Tom's arrival. He remained slouched on his bunk as the young inventor pulled a chair up to the cell bars. His only response was a slight curl of the lips.

"Have you heard about my country's new submarine?" Mirov inquired after Chief Slater left.

Victor Appleton

Tom nodded curtly.

"When are *you* going to build one?" Mirov prodded slyly.

"Look!" Tom snapped. "You asked to see me. Here I am. What is it you want?"

Mirov shrugged with a look of amusement. "To make a bargain with you," he replied casually. "I know the secret of that sub. Get me and my friends released and I'll give it to you."

Tom had no intention of doing so, but he parried the offer, hoping to draw Mirov out further. The prisoner, however, would say nothing more.

At last Tom gave up and rose to leave. "I'll think over your proposition," he said.

He heard Mirov chuckle as he walked away. Somewhat puzzled, Tom reported the conversation to Chief Slater and also telephoned the plant to inform Ames.

Then he hurried back to the car. Bud frowned upon hearing Tom's story.

"Do you think he's on the level?"

Tom shrugged as they headed out into the countryside. "I may be wrong, but the whole thing sounded fishy."

"Now look!" Sandy said severely. "If we're going to enjoy this hike, we're *not* going to talk about Brungarians or inventions or that lost missile. From now on, it will cost anyone five cents every time he breaks the rule!"

The boys chuckled and agreed. But agreeing proved easier than keeping the rule. Again and again, either Tom or Bud would inadvertently drop a remark about their submarine experiments or the search in the South Atlantic. By the time they had parked in the hills and started climbing, Sandy's and Phyl's pockets were jingling with coins.

"What are you going to do with it all?" Bud asked jokingly.

"*Give it to us!*" snapped a strange voice.

As the four young people turned with a start, they saw two men burst from the shrubbery just behind them.

Both were holding guns!

CHAPTER XVI

THE GUNMAN'S SURPRISE

Sandy and Phyl were terrified by the sudden appearance of the rough-looking pair with their drawn revolvers. Tom and Bud remained cool, eying the men warily.

"What's the big idea?" Tom asked.

"Shut up and hoist your mitts!" the bigger of the men snarled. As the boys obeyed, he muttered to his partner, "Keep these two punks covered, Mugs, while I take their cash!"

"Right, Packy! I'll watch 'em!"

Sandy and Phyl emptied their pockets. Then Packy took the boys' wallets and change.

"Now turn around and march!" Packy snapped.

Bud took the lead, followed by the two girls, with Tom bringing up the rear. They plodded up the brushy slope in silence for several minutes. Presently a weather-beaten cabin in a grove of trees came into view.

"You intend to hold us there?" Tom asked.

"You'll find out soon enough!" Packy answered. "We'll teach you to interfere with the Mirovs!"

The Mirovs! Like pieces of a jigsaw puzzle, the whole picture suddenly fell into place. It was clear to Tom now how the capture had been arranged.

The call to the jail from Dimitri Mirov had been a hoax. Its purpose had really been to get Tom away from Enterprises - thus giving the two thugs a starting point from which to follow him. The mountain hike, organized by Bud and the girls, had played right into their hands! As Tom sized up the situation, seeking a way out, the group reached the cabin.

"What are your terms for letting us go?" Tom asked their captors, stalling for time.

The man named Packy gave an ugly chuckle. "None yet," he said. "We may just decide to set the cabin on fire."

Sandy uttered a gasp as his words sank home. Phyl Newton had turned deathly pale. Packy now told his partner to unlock the cabin. Mugs stepped to the door.

At that moment Tom caught Bud's eye. *It was now or never!*

Tom whirled and smashed a stiff handblow to Packy's wrist, knocking the gun from his hand. Bud hurled himself on Mugs.

Taken off guard, the shorter thug staggered and went down under a hail of punches. Bud grabbed his wrist and twisted it mercilessly while he pinned him to the ground.

Mugs screeched with pain. "C-c-cut it out!"

"Then drop your gun!" Bud snapped.

Tom, meanwhile, had followed up his first advantage with a stunning blow to the solar plexus. Packy grunted for breath, then came back viciously with several well-aimed punches that staggered Tom.

As the young inventor stumbled backward, Packy dived for his gun. Though still groggy, Tom managed to kick the weapon out of reach. Before Packy could straighten up, Tom followed with a sweeping uppercut that caught him squarely on the chin.

Packy went down like a felled tree!

Tom picked up the gun before his groaning victim could recover. By this time, Bud had pounded his own opponent into submission. Within a few moments, both thugs were lined up against the wall of the cabin. Their wrists were tightly strapped behind them with their own belts.

"Oh ... thank goodness!" Sandy gasped.

Tom gave the girls a reassuring grin. "Are you two all right?"

"I g-guess so." Phyl gave a nervous smile.

Now that the tables were turned, it was the thugs' turn to "march." The boys herded them warily back down the hillside toward the road, where Bud had parked his red convertible. Sandy and Phyl followed close behind.

Like all cars belonging to the Swifts' key personnel, Bud's was equipped with a two-way shortwave radio. Tom switched it on and radioed Shopton Police Headquarters. Chief Slater promised to send a squad car at once.

Minutes later, they heard it approaching. Two husky police officers leaped out as the car braked to a halt, and took charge of the prisoners. Scowling and sullen, they were driven off to jail.

"Well," said Bud jokingly, "what about that relaxing hike we were starting?"

Phyl sighed. "I'm afraid you two boys just can't get away from *in*ventions and *ad*ventures."

Sandy added, "I suggest we go home for a nice safe dinner."

Later, at the Swifts' house, Tom received a telephone call from Chief Slater. He reported that the two prisoners were known hoodlums from a nearby city.

"They claim they were hired for this job last night by a stranger who spoke with an accent," Slater went on. "According to their story, they never even got a look at his face, and they had no idea he was an enemy agent."

"Sounds reasonable," Tom agreed. "It's not likely Mirov's Brungarian henchmen would endanger their whole setup by taking any cheap gunmen into their confidence."

Chief Slater also reported that Len Unger was still at large. "But the FBI will probably pick him up soon," he added.

"I sure hope so," Tom said.

A ten-hour sleep that night proved a fine tonic. Tom awoke the next morning feeling entirely refreshed, and after a hearty breakfast, hurried off to the plant. Here he plunged into work on his quality analyzer sonar.

Much of the circuitry was assigned to the electronics department. The finished boards and sub-assemblies were fed back to Tom in his private laboratory. He himself assembled the major units.

At lunchtime, over a bowl of chili and crackers, Tom recalled another problem. "We'll need an undetectable sub to test my analyzer," he mused. "That means a repeat job of rigging all those transducers. Whew! I'd better get busy on that plastic sheathing."

As soon as he had eaten, Tom phoned Arv Hanson, who

arrived at the lab in a few moments.

"You remember that idea I mentioned to Danny about molding all the transducers into a single continuous plastic sheet?" As Arv nodded, Tom went on, "Let's try it, using Tomasite as the plastic."

Tom picked up a pencil and quickly sketched out the production steps. By machine-spacing the transmitting and the receiving transducers as closely together as possible, with minimum clearance, the plastic coating could do an even better job of absorbing sonar pings than the hand-rigged model.

"And the leads from all the transducers can be combined into a single flat tape," Tom ended. "That'll make it simple to hook up with the electronic control unit inside."

"Got it, skipper," Arv said tersely. "It'll take overtime to set up the job in the plastics department. But we ought to be rolling out the sheeting Tuesday."

"That's swell, Arv! Thanks!"

By midmorning Tuesday, Tom had his quality analyzer sonar completed and was showing Bud how the units worked.

"Boy, it looks simple enough the way you explain it, prof!" Bud said admiringly. "How soon can we try it?"

"Depends on Arv," Tom replied. He picked up the phone and called the plastics department. To his delight, the sheathing was already being rolled out in quantity. Arv promised that by noon he would have enough of it available to coat a jetmarine.

"Nice going!" Tom said. "Shoot it out to the cargo-jet hangar as soon as it's ready!"

Soon after lunch, Tom, Bud, and Arv took off for Fearing

Island. When they arrived at the base, the plastic coating with its myriad tiny "mikes" and "speakers" was speedily applied to a jetmarine under Arv's supervision. Tom, meanwhile, wired the control unit and also installed the analyzer sonar in the *Sea Hound*.

"Want to be 'It' for another underwater game of hide-and-seek?" Tom asked Bud with a grin.

"Sure, but don't tag me with a torpedo!"

Minutes later, the jetmarine slipped off into the depths with Bud and two other crewmen aboard. Tom and Arv followed in the seacopter. The quality analyzer sonar worked even better than Tom had hoped. He not only tracked the jetmarine on its outward course, but located it three different times after shutting off the analyzer long enough for Bud to seek a new location.

"How'd you like to relieve Hank in the South Atlantic?" Tom asked Bud upon their return.

Bud gave a whoop of excitement. "Roger!"

Tom slapped him on the back. "You can take off as soon as your ship's provisioned. I'll join you later - but first," Tom added mysteriously, "I have another job to attend to."

CHAPTER XVII

A MISSING AMULET

Bud's curiosity was instantly aroused. "Don't tell me you have a new trick up your nautical sleeve to fox the Brungarians?"

Tom grinned. "That's the general idea. I hope to give hydrolung divers the same protection that your jetmarine has."

"You mean make them invisible to sonar?"

"Yes," Tom replied, "and also give them personal spy gear to probe the waters around them and spot an 'undetectable' enemy."

Bud whistled. "Do that, and I'll say you're *really* a magician, skipper!"

Tom himself transferred the analyzer from the *Sea Hound* to Bud's jetmarine. On a chance that it might become necessary to operate at greater depths - either in searching for the lost missile or in shadowing the enemy - Tom also assigned Arv Hanson the job of rigging the *Sea Hound* and another seacopter with his new inventions.

Four crewmen volunteered for the cruise. When the jetmarine was ready, Tom and Bud exchanged tight handshakes.

"Good luck!"

"Thanks, Tom."

The young inventor waved as Bud disappeared down the hatch. As soon as the craft had submerged, Tom went back to Shopton. That evening the Swifts were enjoying a quiet dinner at home when a loud, growling buzz shattered their mealtime conversation.

"Oh!" Sandy gasped. "The burglar alarm!"

The Swifts' house and grounds were protected by a secret magnetic field. Any intruder breaking the barrier touched off the automatic alarm system. To avoid the buzzing, the family and their close friends wore wrist watches containing tiny neutralizer coils.

"I'll see who it is," Tom said, and hurried to the door, feeling a twinge of apprehension.

Was this a new attempt by Brungarian agents?

He switched on the porch light and peered out cautiously through the one-way glass pane in the door. A slim, hatless figure in a dark suit was just coming up the steps. Tom gave a smile of relief.

It was Harlan Ames!

"Hi, Harlan!" Tom opened the door before Ames had a chance to ring the doorbell. "We heard you coming!"

The security chief was startled when he realized he had activated the alarm system.

"That's strange," he said uneasily. "Tom, I wonder if -"

He broke off to dart a quick glance at his wrist. Then his face relaxed into a look of chagrin.

"Great! I forgot my wrist watch!" he murmured. "Haven't visited your house in so long I neglected to wear it."

The other Swifts smiled in amused relief, and Mrs. Swift invited him to join them for dessert. Ames, however, declined politely.

"Thank you, but I just finished dinner myself," he explained. "I dropped by to -"

Once again Ames's voice trailed off in midsentence, as he reached into the side pocket of his coat.

"My amulet!" he gasped. "It's gone!"

"Are you sure?" Tom said with quick concern.

Ames nodded as he frantically tried all his other pockets. The electronic amulet to which he referred had been issued to all Enterprises personnel and family visitors who used the private gate. The amulets were contained in slender bracelets and were designed to trap radar impulses. This prevented them from showing up as blips on the giant detector radarscope mounted on the main building. The purpose of the scope was to reveal unauthorized visitors or spies.

"My bracelet broke this afternoon," Ames said. "I slipped it into my pocket to have it repaired. But it's not there now!"

Tom grabbed a flashlight and dashed outside for a hasty check of the walk. Ames followed, to look inside his black sedan. But the amulet did not come to light.

"Did you go home after you left the plant today?" Tom asked.

Ames shook his head worriedly. "No, I stopped at a restaurant. Mind if I use your phone?"

"Go ahead."

The security chief called Enterprises and asked his assistant, Phil Radnor, who was on night duty, to make a thorough search. While awaiting the results, Ames also called the restaurant, but learned that no such item had been turned in.

Half an hour later Radnor called back to report no luck. "The amulet may show up yet, Harlan," he said. "But I'll alert the guards at the plant to be on the lookout for an unauthorized visitor."

"Thanks, Phil." Ames hung up and turned away from the telephone with an embarrassed look. "Fine example I'm setting as head of plant security," he murmured. "Let's hope the amulet wasn't stolen."

Excusing themselves from Mrs. Swift and Sandy, Tom Sr. and Jr. retired with Ames to Mr. Swift's study to discuss the news he had brought.

"I had a late call from Admiral Walter this evening," Ames explained. "The Navy's getting pretty desperate over that lost missile. They're ready to co-operate with any moves you care to make. I take it you're prepared to carry out a search on your own, Tom?"

The young inventor nodded. "Yes, as soon as I've perfected all the gear I'll need - which won't be long, I hope."

Ames added, unhappily, that certain papers and news commentators had been making snide remarks about the Swifts' failure to match the Brungarians' submarine achievement.

"I think Tom has that situation pretty well in hand," Mr. Swift remarked with a smile.

Tom gave Ames a full report on his own apparatus for rendering a submarine invisible to underwater detection. Ames grinned at the news. The grin grew even wider as he heard of the successful test of the quality analyzer sonar.

"Bud Barclay's on his way to the South Atlantic right now with a fully equipped jetmarine," Tom ended.

The next morning he eagerly tackled the job of adding sonar protection and sonar detection features to his electronic hydrolung. What an amazing fish man the wearer would be, Tom thought, if his project succeeded!

It would enable a skin diver to operate indefinitely under water at jet-propelled speed - invisible to enemy "eyes," yet be able to spy out any hostile undersea prowlers, including supposedly "undetectable" submarines!

Tom chuckled wryly as he mulled over the difficulties ahead. "Bud wasn't kidding when he said it would take a magician!"

Besides his mask, electronic breathing device, density-control unit, and ion drive, the wearer would now need at least three major additions - first, sonar-blinding equipment with electronic control; second, amplifying equipment to camouflage the wearer's noise under water; and, third, a portable quality analyzer sonar.

"Whew! The miniaturizing job alone will be a king-sized headache!" Tom said to himself. "I'd better start with a skin-diving suit made of that molded plastic Arv is turning out."

After having some of the Tomasite sheathing, with its embedding transducers, sent over from the plastics department, Tom cut out a suit from a pattern and welded the seams electronically. He had just finished wiring the control unit when Chow wheeled in a lunch cart.

"Got some *dee*licious steak-and-kidney pie today," the cook announced, setting it out.

"Swell," Tom said absent-mindedly.

Chow frowned but left without interrupting the young

inventor. Twenty minutes later the cook poked his head into the laboratory again. Tom had not yet touched his lunch.

"Brand my vitaminnies, start eatin', boss!"

"Sure, Chow."

By this time, however, Tom had become so absorbed in the task of assembling some tiny monolithic blocks for the computer circuits of his analyzer, that the lunch remained untasted. When Chow returned a third time, Tom was startled by his bellow:

"Get your nose out o' that work, buckaroo, and *eat*!"

Realizing Tom's pie had cooled off, Chow had brought another serving, hot from the oven. Seeing the stern look on the Texan's face, Tom burst out laughing and obeyed meekly.

"I declare!" Chow chuckled. "One o' these days I'll have to force-feed you if you won't pay no mind to your own nourishment!"

"Sorry, old-timer." Tom smiled. "Sometimes I do get a bit wrapped up, I guess."

Hour after hour, Tom stayed glued to his workbench, sometimes busy with delicate electronic gear, sometimes lost in thought as he pondered a tricky problem in circuit design. It was long after dark when he drove home from the experimental station, yet he was back on the job in his laboratory early the next morning.

By lunchtime Tom had all the apparatus assembled. He was just trying on the plastic suit, with all its accompanying paraphernalia, when Chow made his usual appearance.

"Great sufferin' snakes!" the cook gasped. "You ain't goin' divin' in *that* getup, I hope! You look like a Christmas tree, boss!"

Tom nodded glumly. "Know something, Chow? That's just what I was thinking myself."

The young inventor's suit was loaded down with the various electronic units and festooned with wires. Even taking a few steps around the lab convinced Tom that the design was too unwieldy.

"I'd probably either get tangled in seaweed or sink from sheer weight," he muttered.

Changing back to his slacks and T shirt, Tom began eating abstractedly as Chow hovered around.

"If fishes could talk, I reckon you'd scare 'em half to death in that rig!" Chow said, trying to cheer Tom.

"Fish do talk," the young inventor said. "At least they make noises. Don't you remember that emergency fish-talk code we used when we were -"

Suddenly Tom paused, his mouth dropping open. "*Chow!* You've just solved my problem!" he exclaimed.

"I have?" Chow goggled at the young inventor.

"You sure have!" Tom bounced off his stool and began pacing about. "Now, take porpoises. They utter all sorts of sounds - grunts, squeals, jawclaps - and one particularly characteristic sound, like the grating of a rusty hinge."

Chow scratched his chin uncertainly. "Wal, what about it?"

"Suppose I used that rusty-hinge noise to mask the diver's noise." Tom turned and stabbed the air with his finger. "I could *also* use that same sound output as the search pulse for my quality analyzer sonar!"

In this way, Tom explained, he could eliminate part of his bulky equipment and do an even better job of making the diver "invisible."

Bubbling with enthusiasm, Tom decided to buy a live porpoise at once and make an exact recording of its sounds. As soon as he had finished lunch, he put in a number of calls to suppliers of marine specimens. But none could provide a porpoise on short notice.

"Guess I'll have to catch one myself!" Tom told Chow.

He drove out to the airfield and took off in a Whirling Duck for Fearing Island. At the base, both Mel Flagler and Zimby Cox were eager to accompany the young inventor when he told them about the trip he had in mind.

Tom chose the *Sea Hound* as the fastest and best suited craft for his purpose. With Mel's and Zimby's help, he quickly rigged a plastic "tank" in the stern cabin. Minutes later, the seacopter zoomed skyward, heading for the Florida Keys.

The flight was a short one at transonic speed. Tom chose a sparkling stretch of open water, a mile or so offshore from a palm-green islet. Zimby agreed to stay aboard and tend ship while Tom and Mel went over the side in hydrolungs.

The two glided about in the translucent blue depths, keeping in close range of each other. The sea was alive with shimmering fish of every hue, darting among the coral. Suddenly, as Tom veered around to rejoin Mel, his eyes widened in horror.

A vicious-looking hammerhead shark was zeroing in, directly behind his friend!

"Look out!" Tom yelled over his microphone.

CHAPTER XVIII

SMILEY THE SEA COW

Mel turned in the nick of time. The monster shark was bearing down on him like an undersea express train. Overcoming a moment of panic, Mel gunned his ion drive to dodge the attack.

As Tom watched in agonized suspense, he saw the shark's jaws open and shut in a lightning snap at Mel's outstretched arm. Its razor-sharp teeth missed their target by inches!

Mel's gasp of relief was audible over Tom's earphones. "Let's get out of here!" he cried, arrowing away from the man-killer.

Suddenly Tom realized the full extent of their peril. A long, sweeping coral reef, which extended above water, lay between them and the *Sea Hound*. Unless they could round the reef in time, the shark had them trapped!

"Quick! This way!" Tom exclaimed.

The shark was moving at blinding speed. As if sensing the boys' plan of escape, it launched itself in a wide curving sweep to cut them off.

"We can't make it!" Tom gasped. "We'll have to fight!"

Both swimmers were armed with skin diver's knives as a

precaution. The two maneuvered to meet the killer's onslaught.

This time its broad nightmarish head was aiming straight at Tom. He jetted off to the right, but the monster veered instantly. Its lashing tail gave Mel a stunning blow.

As the shark's jaws gaped for a bite, Tom zoomed underneath the man-eater and slashed its belly with his knife.

The shark, maddened, thrashed the water in a frenzy. Tom moved like lightning to dodge a deadly blow from its bony tail. Again and again they felt the horrifying brush of the killer's fins or armor-tough hide. By this time, Mel had revived. Repeatedly the two boys dived to jab and slash at the shark's soft underbelly.

Both were nearly exhausted when the monster at last went limp and floated slowly up toward the surface. Pale with shock and fright, Tom and Mel jetted back to the *Sea Hound*.

Zimby Cox was startled by their faces when they clambered aboard and ripped off their masks. "What happened to you two?"

Tom told him. "Good night!" Zimby cried out.

After resting, Tom and Mel dived in again. This time luck was with them. In less than twenty minutes they sighted a small porpoise.

"Think we can lure it back toward the *Sea Hound*?" Mel queried.

"We'll try," Tom replied.

The creature with the bottle-shaped snout was as friendly and playful as most of its fellow dolphins. Too playful, Tom concluded, after vainly trying to tease it into chasing them.

Instead of following, it would "tag" Tom or Mel quickly, then swim away, evidently expecting to be chased in turn!

"I give up!" Mel snorted in disgust.

Tom grinned and bobbed to the surface. He waved his hand several times in a prearranged signal. Zimby at last spotted him and brought the *Sea Hound* to the scene.

Raising his mask, Tom called, "Let's have the net!"

Zimby lowered a nylon net and some pieces of fish to the two swimmers as they came alongside. With the food as bait they tried to lure the porpoise to the seacopter. But just as they thought they had it, the monster would scoot off.

"It's just laughing at us!" Mel fumed.

At last, after winning its confidence with several bits of fish, the boys succeeded in snaring the porpoise. Tom clambered onto the *Sea Hound*'s deck and helped Zimby haul their catch aboard. "Quacking" reproachfully, it was lowered through the hatch and placed in the tank, which was then pumped full of salt water.

As soon as the *Sea Hound* arrived at Fearing, Tom phoned Chow Winkler at Enterprises and asked him to fly out to the base.

"Pardner, how'd you like to ride herd on this critter and gentle it down for me?" Tom asked, when he showed Chow the porpoise.

It had been transferred to a huge, glass-paneled tank which had been set up just outside Tom's Fearing Island laboratory during his flight to the Florida Keys.

"Reckon I kin try makin' friends with it," Chow declared.

The porpoise stared morosely at Chow. The kindly old Texan's heart was touched by the odd creature. To his delight, it soon responded to his friendly overtures and quickly recovered its good nature. By the next morning the porpoise was playing catch with Chow, or else swimming over to have its back scratched. The cook named it Smiley.

"She's kind of a sea cow," he told Tom, "and you got to talk to my Smiley like any cow!" Tom grinned and refrained from explaining to Chow that a real "sea cow" was a walrus.

Meanwhile, the young inventor was busy with his own experiments. By means of a microphone placed in the tank, he made exact recordings of Smiley's "talk." Using Mel Flagler as a subject, Tom also tape-recorded the sound of a skin diver propelled through the water by ion drive.

The next step was to compare the sound pattern of the tapes. Tom filtered out the difference in the two sounds with the correlation calculator unit of one of his quality analyzer sonars.

"Uh-huh. So you got the difference betwixt Smiley's talk an' the noise Mel made," muttered Chow as he watched the jagged lines of light flashing on the pulse-check oscilloscope. "Now what're you fixin' to do with it?"

"This will be fed into the diver's sonar along with his own noise output," Tom said, "to make him sound like a porpoise."

Chow howled. "That I've got to hear!"

The young inventor worked feverishly throughout the day and into the next, perfecting his new "porpoise sonar." Using microelectronic components, he was able to reduce all the units to amazingly small size.

Next, Tom began tailoring himself a completely new skin-diving suit. Mask, ion-drive jet, and the various hydrolung units were molded into the plastic, with no loose wires or tubes showing.

Monday morning he was ready to try the outfit. The sonarscope with its tiny viewing screen was strapped to his left forearm. Another small unit was fastened to the inside of his wrist, with four plungers in finger-tip reach.

"What in tarnation's that?" Chow asked.

"Simplified controls," Tom explained. "One's for breathing adjustment, one's for the density unit, one is my ion-drive 'throttle,' and this last is for the sonar pulse - which will duplicate the porpoise sound."

The suit worked perfectly in a tank test. Chow was amazed as he listened to Tom gliding about, via an underwater microphone.

"If that don't beat all!" he declared. "Can't tell the difference 'twixt you an' Smiley!"

As Tom emerged from the tank, the portly cook rolled up his own pantlegs and waddled up the metal ladder to the tank brim. He summoned the porpoise with a whistle and straddled its back.

"What in the name of aquanautics do you think *you're* doing?" Tom gasped.

"I'll show you a real broncobustin' act in the water," Chow bragged.

Smiley glided off gently at first, Chow fanning the air with his hat and yipping like a rodeo star. He did, in fact, cling to his slippery perch with considerable skill.

But suddenly Smiley began bobbing and humping like an eel. Chow's face froze in alarm. A moment later the porpoise dived and the cook let out a yell of terror, "He-e-elp!"

Roaring with laughter, Tom dived in and rescued him. "Guess he ain't quite broke yet, pardner!"

"Reckon not."

Now that Tom had all his technical problems solved, he plunged eagerly into the job of fitting out his expedition to the South Atlantic to search for the lost Jupiter missile.

Besides the *Sea Hound* and the other diving seacopter which had already been rigged with antisonar and antidetection equipment, Tom ordered a large cargo jetmarine to be similarly equipped.

Then he drew up a list of supplies and underwater search gear needed for the missile hunt. Tom phoned orders to a dozen different departments. Food, space-plant pills, extra clothing, tools, including a midget atomic earth blaster, grappling hooks - nothing was overlooked.

"I'd better take along a Damonscope too," Tom reflected. "Judging by those Navy reports, ordinary Geiger counters haven't revealed anything."

Tom's Damonscope, one of his early inventions, was a photographic device which worked on fluorescent principles. It was amazingly sensitive to any form of radioactivity - and the missile, of course, would be "hot" from exposure to cosmic rays.

Meanwhile, Tom had ordered his new hydrolung suit, with its four-plunger control unit and porpoise sonar, to be flown back to Enterprises. Arv Hanson had promised to make up several duplicates with a team of technicians working on all-night shifts.

Late the next afternoon Tom returned to the mainland to

Victor Appleton

confer with his father. Mr. Swift reviewed the expedition plans with approval.

"Suppose we call Admiral Walter now and set a time for the Navy to move out of the missile area, so you can take over," his father said.

Tom agreed, and his father placed the long-distance call to Washington. Moments later, Admiral Walter came on the line. Mr. Swift talked to him briefly, then turned the phone over to Tom, who described his preparations for the missile hunt. A time schedule of operations and communications was quickly laid out.

The admiral was amazed to learn that Bud Barclay was already patrolling the area. "Our ships haven't seen or heard him!" the officer exclaimed. Suddenly Admiral Walter broke off. "Hold it, please, Tom! A code call is just coming in!"

His voice was grave as he returned to the Swifts' line. "That message was from your friend, Bud Barclay," Admiral Walter reported. "It looks as if our enemy has found the missile!"

"Oh, no!" Tom groaned.

CHAPTER XIX

FLASH FROM THE DEPTHS

Tom was stunned by the news. "There's no chance of a mistake?"

"Judge for yourself," Admiral Walter replied. He read the message:

HAVE JUST SIGHTED ENEMY CRAFT DREDGING OUT METAL OBJECT

Tom repeated the information to his father. Both Swifts were silent for a moment, exchanging dejected looks. Then Mr. Swift remarked evenly:

"The game's never lost till it's over, son."

"You're right, Dad!" Tom exclaimed. Turning back to the telephone, he said, "Admiral, I'm not quitting. We'll take off as soon as I can get back to the base!"

With a hasty good-by to his father, and farewells to his mother, Sandy, and Phyl by phone, Tom dashed out of the building. He sped to Arv Hanson's workshop, and the new hydrolung suits were loaded onto a small pickup truck and taken to the airfield. While flying back to Fearing Island in a helijet, Tom received a radio flash from his father.

Victor Appleton

"Another message from Bud. He says the object dug up by the Brungarians was *not* the missile. It appeared to be the metal section of a ship's prow, from some hulk buried in the silt!"

Tom was jubilant. "Terrific news, Dad! Our luck may be turning!"

At the rocket base Tom detailed crews for the three undersea craft which were to take off on the expedition. Arv Hanson would captain one seacopter, Mel Flagler the jetmarine, while Zimby Cox, Chow, and four crewmen would accompany Tom in the *Sea Hound.*

Because of their sonar-blinding systems, Tom realized there was a chance of the ships losing contact with one another - especially if their analyzer sonars developed trouble. He therefore plotted their course to the South Atlantic carefully, and issued orders for the antidetection circuits to be switched off every half-hour for a position check.

"Report to your ships," he now ordered.

As Tom was about to leave base headquarters, Harlan Ames telephoned from Shopton. "Bad news, Tom. Dimitri Mirov has broken jail!"

"Good night!" Tom stifled a groan of dismay. "How did it happen?"

Ames said the Brungarian had somehow fashioned a crude weapon and overpowered the turnkey. Disguising himself in the guard's uniform, he had slipped out before his victim was discovered.

"He must have had outside help within close call," Ames ended, "because he seems to have made a clean getaway. The State Police have spread a dragnet, but it doesn't look hopeful."

"He'll probably duck out of the country pronto," Tom surmised. "Anyhow, this won't stop us, Harlan."

By nightfall the little fleet of three undersea craft was speeding southward at periscope depth. Tom alternated at the controls with Zimby, two hours on and two hours off. Sleep came in snatches, the crewmen flopping on their bunks as the chance offered. Chow's tasty meals helped break the monotony.

It was the following day when they reached the missile search area. Tom surfaced the *Sea Hound* and reversed blade pitch, then gunned the rotor turbines for an aerial reconnaissance flight, while the jetmarine and the other seacopter stood by in the water.

"Brand my guppies, it's some ocean, eh, boss?" Chow remarked in an awed voice.

"Big enough, all right," Tom agreed with a grin. "And plenty of water to search in."

"No sign of the Navy," Zimby said.

Tom nodded. "They pulled out on schedule."

"What about them Brungarian sidewinders?" put in Chow.

"That's the question!" Tom swooped down to rejoin the other two craft. "We'll keep an eye out for enemy blips while we do our prospecting."

Rather than lose time trying to contact Bud, Tom decided to let him find the *Sea Hound*. Accordingly, he switched off the antidetection system and ordered all ships to submerge. Arv's seacopter and Mel's jetmarine were to maintain close formation and stand guard while Tom's craft did the actual searching.

Now the missile hunt began. Tom had plotted a concentric

search pattern, focused on the probable position worked out by the task-force computers. After checking his fix on the automatic navigator, Tom switched on the Damonscope and steered the *Sea Hound* on a gradually circling course.

The Damonscope was mounted in a blister on the hull, its camera lens pointing toward the ocean floor. The automatic developing film would record any trace of fluorescence, and a red light would signal this result to the pilot's cabin.

Minutes went by as the *Sea Hound* nosed slowly along through the gray-green gloom, its sister craft flanking it a hundred yards on either side. They were moving only a fathom or so above the bottom.

"A blip at eleven o'clock!" the sonarman called out suddenly. Tom's pulse quickened. "Moving straight toward us," the sonarman added.

Tom surrendered the controls to Zimby long enough to dart over and study the sonarscope. "I've a hunch it's Bud," he told the others.

His guess proved correct when the unmistakable outline of a jetmarine loomed into view. Tom flicked on the search beam for a moment, and Bud could be seen waving through the cabin window. Then the yellow glare went off, and Bud's jetmarine glided away to take up a scouting position ahead of the *Sea Hound*.

An hour went by, then another. Suddenly a flash of light stabbed through the murk from dead ahead.

"It's a signal from Bud!" Zimby exclaimed.

Tom nodded grimly. "He's spotted trouble - probably an enemy sub." Silence settled over the cabin as Tom reached out to switch on the antisonar circuits.

At that same instant a red light flashed on the control panel. "The Damonscope!" Tom cried out. "We may be over the Jupiter prober!"

Cutting off the steering jets, Tom gave a brief flick on the reverse jets to halt the craft. Then he turned over the controls to Zimby and began stripping down to don a hydrolung suit.

"Gallopin' guppies! What're you aimin' to do?" Chow exploded.

"Go out and look for that missile," Tom said calmly. "It's what we came for."

"Are you loco, boss? What about that sub Bud just spotted? Mebbe it's Mirov's bunch!"

Tom refused to be dissuaded. After swallowing a space-plant pill, he armed himself with an underwater flashlight.

"Think it's safe to show that light, skipper?" a crewman asked uneasily.

"If the enemy spots it, I'm hoping they'll think it's coming from a school of lantern fish or sea anglers," Tom explained. He picked up a three-pronged digging fork with his other hand and went out through the air lock.

Tom glided back to the spot which the *Sea Hound* had just passed over and began digging into the silt. Presently he felt the fork strike something hard.

"An obstruction!" Tom thought excitedly.

He probed deeper. Bit by bit, a smoothly contoured and still-shiny metal surface became visible. "I've found it!" Tom's eyes flashed in triumph, his heart pounding.

There was no doubt he had uncovered the nose cone of the

Victor Appleton

missile which had re-entered the earth's atmosphere tailfirst!

Meanwhile, Bud, keeping watch on the enemy submarine, had seen a shadowy figure glide from its air lock and head in Tom's direction. Bud donned a hydrolung and followed.

"What's that he's carrying?" Bud wondered.

Suddenly the answer came to him - a self-propelled underwater grenade! Horrified, Bud jetted forward, tackling the diver at full speed.

A split second too late! The grenade went streaking straight toward Tom Swift!

CHAPTER XX

A LUCKY BLAST

Tom's earphones caught the hiss of the approaching grenade. Instantly his eyes darted to the sonarscope on his wrist.

A tiny blip of light was moving on the screen!

Tom whirled about, then gunned his ion drive. He pushed out of the path of the grenade, which nevertheless grazed him as it streaked past.

Seconds later, the grenade struck bottom. A shattering *bo-o-oom* reverberated through the depths, and clouds of silt darkened the water into Stygian gloom.

Tom, knocked off balance, was tumbled about helplessly by the train of shock waves. As they died away, he gradually recovered his bearings and pressed the throttle control of his ion drive. It coughed and stuttered! For a moment Tom felt a surge of panic, but the jet motor smoothed into a steady purr of power.

"Whew!" he thought in relief. "At least I can still get around at full speed if anything else comes at me!"

He had clung to the flashlight and fork despite the explosion. The blast had hurled him away from the spot where the missile was buried, so Tom began trying to locate it again.

But he soon realized that his efforts were hopeless. He must wait until the silt which clouded the water cleared. Now Tom feared that the explosion might have reburied the nose cone.

Suddenly a new worry gripped him. *Had the missile's precious contents been destroyed by the blast?!* Slowly he began making his way back to the *Sea Hound*.

Unknown to Tom, Bud was fighting a desperate battle with his adversary barely fifty yards away. The divers grappled each other in an octopuslike duel. At such depths, their movements were impeded, as if by oil.

The Brungarian pulled out the knife at his belt. Bud, a skilled wrestler from high-school days, managed to twist his foe's knife arm behind his back - then applied a punishing judo hold! The Brungarian gave an audible screech of pain and dropped the knife.

"Now you're coming along with me!" Bud muttered. He gunned his jet, forcing himself and his adversary toward the *Sea Hound*.

Moments later, they passed the seacopter's cabin window. Reaching the air lock, Bud hammered for admission. The hatch opened quickly and his prisoner was hauled inside. Bud followed.

Tom greeted him with a bear hug. "Hi, Bud, you old devilfish!" Turning to the prisoner, Tom added "Who's this?"

"The rat who fired that grenade at you!"

The prisoner was wearing a frogman costume and a mask which hid the lower part of his face. The man's dark eyes glittered in hate, as Tom ordered him to remove his mask. Sullenly the prisoner obeyed.

Tom gasped. "*Dimitri Mirov!*" The name sent a shock through the Americans aboard.

"Wal, I'll be jing-whistled!" Chow declared, then broke into a gleeful cackle.

Under their scornful gaze, the Brungarian's own eyes wavered and his shoulders slumped in an attitude of defeat. "What is the use?" he muttered. "Again I have failed. My career is over now, just like my brother's."

Tom seized the opening. "In that case, maybe you're ready to do some talking now."

Mirov shrugged. "What do you wish to know?"

In answer to Tom's questions, Mirov admitted that his group, composed of Brungarian rebel Navy men and rocket engineers, had sabotaged the returning Jupiter probe missile, hoping to obtain its data for their own use.

Their key agent in America was the man who had posed over the phone as Lester Morris and masterminded the other attempts to kidnap Tom. He had also taken the amulet bracelet from Ames's jacket in a restaurant.

Mirov himself had been given the bracelet after his jail break. Pulling back the sleeve of his frogman suit, he displayed it with a momentary smirk of pride.

"I even got inside the grounds of Swift Enterprises and stole a plane that same night," Mirov boasted.

Tom was startled. "How did you manage that?"

"Very simple. I thumbed a ride with one of your trusted workers on the late shift and showed him the amulet to identify myself as a Swift employee. The guard at the gate was fooled the same way."

Tom nodded thoughtfully. "They were instructed to look for a man trying to sneak past alone. Seeing you in the same car with a known employee, he probably assumed you were all right."

Mirov was allowed to change into dry clothes, then his hands were bound behind his back. When the water cleared, Tom and Bud ventured outside again. First they headed for Bud's jetmarine to reassure his crew. Here they learned that the mystery submarine had vanished.

"Good riddance!" Bud exclaimed jubilantly. "They probably didn't even realize you had found the missile!"

"*Had found* is right - past tense," Tom said wryly. "It's no doubt buried again. But at least we have the right spot."

They emerged from the jetmarine and headed back toward the site. As they glided astern of the *Sea Hound*, Tom uttered a cry over his suit mike.

"*Bud! There it is!*"

Both boys darted ahead at increased speed, and Tom played his flashlight beam over the precious treasure. Instead of burying the missile deeper, the grenade explosion had uncovered the entire nose cone and part of the section behind it!

"Sizzlin' squids! What a break!" Bud whooped.

The boys jetted back to the *Sea Hound* to announce the good news. Zimby and two other crewmen were dispatched in hydrolungs to inform the other ships. Tom requested them to remain submerged and guard the site.

Twenty minutes later the *Sea Hound* was zooming up to the surface. Tom hoisted the craft's aerial and radioed word to his father, who was overjoyed. Mr. Swift, in turn, had news - that the rebels' key man and Len Unger had been seized by the

FBI. Tom's next call was to Admiral Walter.

"Tom, this is wonderful news!" the admiral exclaimed. "I'll have our Navy ships routed back there immediately - and I intend to fly out myself as soon as I can board a plane!"

As Tom waited for the task force to arrive, his thoughts turned to new inventions to tackle. But he could not anticipate what would happen to him in his *Triphibian Atomicar.*

Within hours, the task force arrived at the site and recovery operations got under way. The missile was hoisted to the surface by cables attached to submarines, then hauled aboard the tender. Tom himself supervised the job of extracting the sealed data section.

"You've done a tremendous job, Tom Swift, and our whole country will be proud of you!" Admiral Walter declared before sailing home.

Tom grinned as he prepared to descend the ladder over the side. "Let me know about life on Jupiter, sir. I may go there myself one of these days!"

Choose from Thousands of 1stWorldLibrary Classics By

A. M. Barnard
Ada Leverson
Adolphus William Ward
Aesop
Agatha Christie
Alexander Aaronsohn
Alexander Kielland
Alexandre Dumas
Alfred Gatty
Alfred Ollivant
Alice Duer Miller
Alice Turner Curtis
Alice Dunbar
Allen Chapman
Ambrose Bierce
Amelia E. Barr
Amory H. Bradford
Andrew Lang
Andrew McFarland Davis
Andy Adams
Anna Alice Chapin
Anna Sewell
Annie Besant
Annie Hamilton Donnell
Annie Payson Call
Annie Roe Carr
Annonaymous
Anton Chekhov
Arnold Bennett
Arthur Conan Doyle
Arthur M. Winfield
Arthur Ransome
Arthur Schnitzler
Atticus
B.H. Baden-Powell
B. M. Bower
B. C. Chatterjee
Baroness Emmuska Orczy
Baroness Orczy
Basil King
Bayard Taylor
Ben Macomber
Bertha Muzzy Bower
Bjornstjerne Bjornson
Booth Tarkington
Boyd Cable
Bram Stoker
C. Collodi
C. E. Orr

C. M. Ingleby
Carolyn Wells
Catherine Parr Traill
Charles A. Eastman
Charles Amory Beach
Charles Dickens
Charles Dudley Warner
Charles Farrar Browne
Charles Ives
Charles Kingsley
Charles Klein
Charles Hanson Towne
Charles Lathrop Pack
Charles Romyn Dake
Charles Whibley
Charles Willing Beale
Charlotte M. Braeme
Charlotte M. Yonge
Charlotte Perkins Stetson
Clair W. Hayes
Clarence Day Jr.
Clarence E. Mulford
Clemence Housman
Confucius
Coningsby Dawson
Cornelis DeWitt Wilcox
Cyril Burleigh
D. H. Lawrence
Daniel Defoe
David Garnett
Dinah Craik
Don Carlos Janes
Donald Keyhoe
Dorothy Kilner
Dougan Clark
Douglas Fairbanks
E. Nesbit
E.P.Roe
E. Phillips Oppenheim
Earl Barnes
Edgar Rice Burroughs
Edith Van Dyne
Edith Wharton
Edward Everett Hale
Edward J. O'Biren
Edward S. Ellis
Edwin L. Arnold
Eleanor Atkins
Eliot Gregory

Elizabeth Gaskell
Elizabeth McCracken
Elizabeth Von Arnim
Ellem Key
Emerson Hough
Emilie F. Carlen
Emily Dickinson
Enid Bagnold
Enilor Macartney Lane
Erasmus W. Jones
Ernie Howard Pie
Ethel May Dell
Ethel Turner
Ethel Watts Mumford
Eugenie Foa
Eugene Wood
Eustace Hale Ball
Evelyn Everett-green
Everard Cotes
F. H. Cheley
F. J. Cross
F. Marion Crawford
Federick Austin Ogg
Ferdinand Ossendowski
Francis Bacon
Francis Darwin
Frances Hodgson Burnett
Frances Parkinson Keyes
Frank Gee Patchin
Frank Harris
Frank Jewett Mather
Frank L. Packard
Frank V. Webster
Frederic Stewart Isham
Frederick Trevor Hill
Frederick Winslow Taylor
Friedrich Kerst
Friedrich Nietzsche
Fyodor Dostoyevsky
G.A. Henty
G.K. Chesterton
Gabrielle E. Jackson
Garrett P. Serviss
Gaston Leroux
George A. Warren
George Ade
Geroge Bernard Shaw
George Durston
George Ebers

George Eliot
George Gissing
George MacDonald
George Meredith
George Orwell
George Sylvester Viereck
George Tucker
George W. Cable
George Wharton James
Gertrude Atherton
Gordon Casserly
Grace E. King
Grace Gallatin
Grace Greenwood
Grant Allen
Guillermo A. Sherwell
Gulielma Zollinger
Gustav Flaubert
H. A. Cody
H. B. Irving
H.C. Bailey
H. G. Wells
H. H. Munro
H. Irving Hancock
H. Rider Haggard
H. W. C. Davis
Haldeman Julius
Hall Caine
Hamilton Wright Mabie
Hans Christian Andersen
Harold Avery
Harold McGrath
Harriet Beecher Stowe
Harry Castlemon
Harry Coghill
Harry Houidini
Hayden Carruth
Helent Hunt Jackson
Helen Nicolay
Hendrik Conscience
Hendy David Thoreau
Henri Barbusse
Henrik Ibsen
Henry Adams
Henry Ford
Henry Frost
Henry James
Henry Jones Ford
Henry Seton Merriman
Henry W Longfellow
Herbert A. Giles

Herbert Carter
Herbert N. Casson
Herman Hesse
Hildegard G. Frey
Homer
Honore De Balzac
Horace B. Day
Horace Walpole
Horatio Alger Jr.
Howard Pyle
Howard R. Garis
Hugh Lofting
Hugh Walpole
Humphry Ward
Ian Maclaren
Inez Haynes Gillmore
Irving Bacheller
Isabel Hornibrook
Israel Abrahams
Ivan Turgenev
J.G.Austin
J. Henri Fabre
J. M. Barrie
J. Macdonald Oxley
J. S. Fletcher
J. S. Knowles
J. Storer Clouston
Jack London
Jacob Abbott
James Allen
James Andrews
James Baldwin
James Branch Cabell
James DeMille
James Joyce
James Lane Allen
James Lane Allen
James Oliver Curwood
James Oppenheim
James Otis
James R. Driscoll
Jane Austen
Jane L. Stewart
Janet Aldridge
Jens Peter Jacobsen
Jerome K. Jerome
John Burroughs
John Cournos
John F. Kennedy
John Gay
John Glasworthy

John Habberton
John Joy Bell
John Kendrick Bangs
John Milton
John Philip Sousa
Jonas Lauritz Idemil Lie
Jonathan Swift
Joseph A. Altsheler
Joseph Carey
Joseph Conrad
Joseph E. Badger Jr
Joseph Hergesheimer
Joseph Jacobs
Jules Vernes
Julian Hawthrone
Julie A Lippmann
Justin Huntly McCarthy
Kakuzo Okakura
Kenneth Grahame
Kenneth McGaffey
Kate Langley Bosher
Kate Langley Bosher
Katherine Cecil Thurston
Katherine Stokes
L. A. Abbot
L. T. Meade
L. Frank Baum
Latta Griswold
Laura Dent Crane
Laura Lee Hope
Laurence Housman
Lawrence Beasley
Leo Tolstoy
Leonid Andreyev
Lewis Carroll
Lewis Sperry Chafer
Lilian Bell
Lloyd Osbourne
Louis Hughes
Louis Tracy
Louisa May Alcott
Lucy Fitch Perkins
Lucy Maud Montgomery
Luther Benson
Lydia Miller Middleton
Lyndon Orr
M. Corvus
M. H. Adams
Margaret E. Sangster
Margret Howth
Margaret Vandercook

Margret Penrose
Maria Edgeworth
Maria Thompson Daviess
Mariano Azuela
Marion Polk Angellotti
Mark Overton
Mark Twain
Mary Austin
Mary Catherine Crowley
Mary Cole
Mary Hastings Bradley
Mary Roberts Rinehart
Mary Rowlandson
M. Wollstonecraft Shelley
Maud Lindsay
Max Beerbohm
Myra Kelly
Nathaniel Hawthrone
Nicolo Machiavelli
O. F. Walton
Oscar Wilde
Owen Johnson
P.G. Wodehouse
Paul and Mabel Thorne
Paul G. Tomlinson
Paul Severing
Percy Brebner
Peter B. Kyne
Plato
R. Derby Holmes
R. L. Stevenson
R. S. Ball
Rabindranath Tagore
Rahul Alvares
Ralph Bonehill
Ralph Henry Barbour
Ralph Victor
Ralph Waldo Emmerson
Rene Descartes
Rex Beach

Rex E. Beach
Richard Harding Davis
Richard Jefferies
Richard Le Gallienne
Robert Barr
Robert Frost
Robert Gordon Anderson
Robert L. Drake
Robert Lansing
Robert Lynd
Robert Michael Ballantyne
Robert W. Chambers
Rosa Nouchette Carey
Rudyard Kipling
Samuel B. Allison
Samuel Hopkins Adams
Sarah Bernhardt
Sarah C. Hallowell
Selma Lagerlof
Sherwood Anderson
Sigmund Freud
Standish O'Grady
Stanley Weyman
Stella Benson
Stella M. Francis
Stephen Crane
Stewart Edward White
Stijn Streuvels
Swami Abhedananda
Swami Parmananda
T. S. Ackland
T. S. Arthur
The Princess Der Ling
Thomas A. Janvier
Thomas A Kempis
Thomas Anderton
Thomas Bailey Aldrich
Thomas Bulfinch
Thomas De Quincey
Thomas Dixon

Thomas H. Huxley
Thomas Hardy
Thomas More
Thornton W. Burgess
U. S. Grant
Valentine Williams
Various Authors
Vaughan Kester
Victor Appleton
Victoria Cross
Virginia Woolf
Wadsworth Camp
Walter Camp
Walter Scott
Washington Irving
Wilbur Lawton
Wilkie Collins
Willa Cather
Willard F. Baker
William Dean Howells
William le Queux
W. Makepeace Thackeray
William W. Walter
William Shakespeare
Winston Churchill
Yei Theodora Ozaki
Yogi Ramacharaka
Young E. Allison
Zane Grey

www.ingramcontent.com/pod-product-compliance
Lightning Source LLC
Chambersburg PA
CBHW020504100426
42813CB00030B/3115/J